THE LIFE AND TIMES OF
DAVE'S SAVING GRACE
The Story of the Worlds Sweetest Dog

Dave's Saving Grace & J.D. Haak

It's nap time. Playing is hard.

The Life & Times of Dave's Saving Grace

Published by: Fine Line Design Publishing with Amazon Publishing

ISBN #9798352076569

US Copyright Registration Number:

TXu 2-311-033

Printed in the United States of America

Cover Design: Weston Hirvela
Contact Instagram: @gun_tale or
Weston.hirvela@gmail.com

Editor: Haden Gross
Thanks to Justice for the connections.

First printing 2022

Disclaimer: This is a true story – you know what that means right? You will cry and laugh and enjoy.

<u>DEDICATION</u>

There are two that truly deserve this dedication.

First is my daughter, the person who brought Gracie into our lives. Thank you for that choice. You gave this family something that we will think of with fondness and great love throughout our lives. For all your love for her, thank you.

Second, Gracie herself: For every moment you knew to come to the side of the one who needed you. For every laugh you gave, for every lesson you taught and needed yourself, for everything, just for everything. Thank you. You made a difference. You were exactly what a dog should be... an unconditional friend, a therapist, a pain in the butt, a money sucker, and most of all, a beautiful gift.

And now her story, in her own words... kinda.

<u>**Contents**</u>

AND THEN YOU CAME

Right on time!

THE EARLY YEARS

Ah, youth.

THERE WERE BUMPS ALONG THE WAY

Ouch!

THE BEST OF TIMES

Memories matter.

WHAT I BROUGHT TO THE WORLD

The good, the bad, and the ugly – wait a minute – I'm not ugly – the good, the bad, the beautiful me.

THE YEARS THEY WANE

The days they are a changin'.

The Life & Times of Dave's Saving Grace

INTRODUCTION

To start with, you need to promise me that like you did when you watched The Wizard of Oz, or Thor Ragnarök (my cousin and gramma love that movie) or A Dog's Journey, you will suspend your reality, because, quite frankly folks, and you know this... dogs still don't talk. Yet with the help of my grandmother, I am going to tell you the story of my life as best I can.

Like any other dog, there is a lot to our lives that you don't know or understand. So, maybe, just maybe, after you read this story, you'll have a little better understanding and appreciation for your own dog, or one that is in your life in some way, or any other pet you may know.

Gramma says that some of the pictures are old, but then some of those memories are old too. I know you'll understand that once upon a time we took photographs, real photographs, but like people and pets, they age too... ha, ha.

So, here we go.

The Life & Times of Dave's Saving Grace

Chapter 1

AND THEN YOU CAME

Right on time!

Look at me, I'ne such a little thing.

The Life & Times of Dave's Saving Grace

First, this is a story… not a tale. The difference? A tale tells you all the exciting things a writer wants for their character, no matter how much imagination they have to use to bring the excitement to the level they want you to feel. A story… a story shows the reality of life, both good and bad. A story is a little truer to life. I hope you enjoy my story.

Let's start at the beginning. After all, I wasn't here before the beginning and the story is about me. I don't remember the exact time, day, or the order I was born… but here I am! I've heard it was August 4, 2002.

I was someplace dark, wet, and warm with some other puppies. They were things like me. Before I knew it, somebody was pushing me out of a long dark tunnel, and I hit the ground. Boom! Seriously… boom! I was born. I think the pup in front of me stepped on my ear, it hurt for a while. The one behind me was shoving me with its foot. Out we came.

Here we are, there's about five or six of us. They all look like the big dog that pushed us out of that long, dark tunnel. Oh my Gosh! She's licking all that wet gunk off us one by one… I am serious... with her tongue! Gross, gross, she's licking us until we're all dry, with her tongue! Then, you're gonna love this, she pulled us up to her and attached us to something that gave us milk. It was great! Next, she pushed us under her big fat belly, and we all fell asleep. What a life. When we woke up, we did it all over again. Can you believe this? It's awesome here.

The Worlds Sweetest Dog

Oh crap! There's a big thing coming at us. It's a man, how do I know that? I just do. I know language, who knew. He's bending down to the big dog that cleaned us off. "So, you're a mother now Belle". He said it like he knows her well. "Six beagle pups." He pets her head and smiles at us. "Good job girl". He stands and walks away, and she goes to sleep. So, we do too… again.

It's been a while since we came out of the cave. We got to eat a few more times. Boy, this is the life. It rained the other day and I strolled into a mud puddle; I saw myself for the first time. I look like the other five that are here… I'm a little cuter than they are, just a little. My markings are a little different. I stand out a little more. My brown markings are darker brown, and my black is really black and the white on my body is usually very clean, usually. I think I'm pretty. I feel pretty.

So, we are beagles, I'm okay with that. Days, weeks have gone by, and we just keep eating, sleeping, pooping, peeing, and playing with each other. It's a good life here on the farm. A farm, what a place to live! Every day we get to play, run, eat, and sleep. What more could you ask for? I laid in the sun the other day for the whole day, nobody cared, so I didn't. I just laid there and let the sun warm my little body.

Today, in an instant, everything about my life will change, everything, absolutely everything. We were playing in the yard; we like to roll in the goose poop in the yard. We get dirty but the farmer always sprays us off, we shake and go right back to it. We were playing very hard and decided to take a nap after he sprayed us off. We were all laying on the lawn, the sun was shining and then it happened. The farmer came up with two people. They looked at all of us and picked every one of us up and looked in our faces. I sneezed and they set me right back down.

Then, for no reason at all, those two people gave the farmer some paper and they kidnapped two of the puppies. We all started barking when they were taking them away and we tried to get him to help them, but he just put the paper in his pocket and walked away. The big dog barked, and he yelled at her to be quiet as he walked in the house. She walked over to the barn, whimpered slightly, and laid down. I think I saw tears come from her eyes. She was so sad and just went to sleep for a long time.

The next day things went back to normal. We played and slept and ate. Life was back to the normal we knew. Then, the next day it happened again. That rotten farmer brought some people with kids out and they rolled us all around and picked us up and hugged us. I sneezed again, it worked, they put me down and turned to another one of the pups. It got annoying after a while. The farmer took paper again and they kidnapped another one of the pups. Now there were only three of us left. The big dog was sad again. She put her head down and walked to the barn. I felt bad for her. Why was this farmer so nice to her before and now he's letting people steal her puppies?

It must have been about a week later when we were all out in the yard enjoying the sunny day and playing with each other. We found a really dirty stick, and all took turns chewing it to pieces. I really enjoy chewing sticks, I always will. We were sitting there watching the tree branches move... all on their own... they must be magic.

Then a vehicle pulls in. I took a deep breath as this beautiful, long legged lady steps out. The farmer walks up and smiles at her as they shake hands. He leads her over to the big dog and she bends down and pets her. I check the area to see if I can escape. My options don't look good as she moves toward the three of us.

She walks right over to me and picks me up. She looks right in my eyes and smiles. Oh no... she likes me. She looks at the other two, still holding me in her arms. I must admit, her body is warm, and she is very caring. Doesn't matter though, I don't wanna leave this place. This is heaven, I'm free, I'm taken care of, this is home. I love it here. I sneeze again, doesn't work this time. She smiles, what... what's wrong with her?

Finally, she sets me down. She walks over and talks to the other two. I don't want them to be kidnapped... but... better them than me. I decided to walk away and hide, but she sees me move and grabs me up again. She kisses my head, ruthless with her affection. I need to get away from her. I squirm, she holds me tighter. She looks at the other two again and looks to the farmer and smiles. He smiles back. I know what this means.

No... no... no. She's handing the farmer paper like the others did. It goes in his pocket and the big beagle and the other two look at me with sorrow as she walks toward her vehicle, me in her arms! Somebody save me... please! She puts me in the seat beside her and I try to get out, but I can't. Oh no, what's going to happen to me?

I'm distraught (I know it's a big word, but apparently, I'm pretty smart). I look up and out the window as she drives away from the farm. This horrible human is taking me away from the only life I have ever known. I know it's only been about six weeks, but it's all I've known. I love it at the farm. Nobody cares if we run, get dirty, play in the mud, lay in the sun, we're free. We eat when we want, and we can poop anywhere we feel like. I know she's going to hurt me. I'm exhausted from fear and sorrow. The vehicle is moving easy, it's mesmerizing as I stretch my neck to look out the window. I can barely see, but we're moving. I'm going to take a nap. Maybe this is just a bad dream.

We stop. I try to look out the window. It's pretty high up. I see a bunch of buildings close to each other. She turns the vehicle off and reaches over to grab me. I have nowhere to go, she scoops me up and we get out. We are headed for one of these buildings. Up the steps we go, me in her arms. I think I'm going to bite her. My brothers and sisters bite me all the time, we all bite each other. It hurts. Maybe if I bite her, she'll drop me and then, I can run back to the farm. I don't know where I am though, I don't know where the farm is.

I missed my chance; she opens the door, we walk in. Oh my Gosh! What is this place? Where am I? This isn't outdoors. I'm a beagle; I must be outdoors. I only know what to do outdoors. There's another person in here like her... a lot older though. She speaks to her. "Her name is Grace".

What? No, it's not, my name is beagle. I'm a beagle. She sets me down as that other lady comes at me. I'll show them... I'll pee. I do. This will make them take me back. Oh no. Long legs scoops me up and the lady wipes up the pee. She scolds me, kindly. I don't know what else to do, they're bigger than me, I can't bite them both at the same time.

The other lady takes me from long legs and kisses me until I can't breathe anymore. These two are very annoying. She asks her where my name came from... cuz I'm a beagle, it's beagle. She tells her it's from a Dave Matthews song, Grace Is Gone. What? That's silly, I don't know Dave Matthews, what's he doing naming me. Whatever, long legs just loves Dave Matthews I guess, crazy girl. Who's Dave Matthews anyhow? What does he know about beagles.

Anyhow, I need to figure a way out. Wait a minute, long legs brings out a bunch of toys and the other one gives me some kind of a treat. It's really good. Maybe I'll give it a day and then plan my escape back to the farm.

I wonder what happened to the other two at the farm. The way it looked; people were going to take all of us from the big beagle. Why? She's the one who brought us into the world. She didn't do anything wrong. How cruel to take all of us away from her. I know she must be so sad at what that farmer did to us. He was so nice to her, until they took the puppies, that was mean.

So, we left her house and went somewhere else. This must be where the long-legged one lives. She seems very comfortable and knows how to use everything in here. She sets me down and draws me to a nice bed. There's lots of toys for me, but I want to go home. There's another person here. I'm not sure I like him. I don't think he'll be here long.

Where am I?

Days have gone by. It's just me, her, and him. She's nice, she loves to cuddle all the time and even though it's still a little annoying, it's kinda nice. She feeds me, takes me outside to pee and poop and play a little. This place is nothing like the farm. Too many buildings around me, I want to go back to the farm. As days go by, she gets nicer and more attentive toward me. She really loves me. I like her, I like her more than I did the day she kidnapped me. She's nice and she takes care of me. There's a ton of toys here and she feeds me well. I guess if I had to be kidnapped, she's a pretty good person to be kidnapped by. I still wanna go home.

Do they know how high this grass is – I could get lost down here.

So, this is me. It's been a few days and we're back at the big old lady's house. This is outside? She puts me down before we go inside. For what, I don't like it here. This is nothing like the farm. There's nowhere to run, there's a bunch of other big buildings here. There are no fields, no mud puddles, no sticks to play with, nobody like me. I'm lost here and I'm not gonna move. I'm gonna sit here until they take me back to the farm. I still miss the farm so much… it was my home. Oh crap, I gotta pee. Now I gotta move.

Inside the other lady has almost as many toys for me as long legs does at her house. I don't know why they like me so much, but they do. These two talk a lot. They go on about a net, a vet, a pet… I don't know what they're talking about. I'm tired and they're not stopping. I'll take a nap. Before I know it, we're back in the vehicle and on our way somewhere else.

We're at another building. Too many buildings. It's not her house. It doesn't look anything like her house. We go inside, she's carrying me because, evidently, I can't walk fast enough for her. Inside there are people behind a desk and she talks with them and then we go sit down. There are other dogs (I guess they're dogs) here. There is something someone called a cat. Yuck, they're goofy looking. Nothing like a dog. I stick my nose out to smell it and it hisses at me and slaps at me with its paw. Somebody get rid of that thing, please! Soon a person comes out and the lady with the cat goes through a door. Awesome, they're going to nix the cat. Then another person comes through the door and looks at my *animal holder*, long legs. She stands and we walk toward the same door the cat went through. Oh no, they're going to nix me.

We walk in a room and long legs sets me on a table. She's not very responsible. I could fall, this table is way off the ground. Doesn't look like the ground, whatever it is, it is far away. If I fall, I won't survive. It'll be all her fault. As I watch the ground below, a man walks through the door. They put me on something and talk about my weight. She tells him I'm eating good and that I love to play. That's all true. She sets me back on the table. The other lady in the room has a treat in her hand. It must be for me. It's the same kind of treats I get at her house. The man in the room has something long and pointed in his hand. I'll take the treat thank you.

Then, as that woman comes at me with the treat, long legs holds me very tight, and that man sticks that pointy thing in my side. OH MY GOSH!!!! OUCH!!! I scream, whimper… whatever. It hurts! It really hurts! I try to jump off the table, but they won't let me. He smiles at me – it's not funny! The lady gives me the treat… I'm whining… but… I want that treat… I take it. It's over… what? Now they're talking about more of these *shots* in the future. No thank you, I'll pass. I won't be having any more of these. I look at long legs and she is smiling as she pets my head. I'll get her back. I'll do something to her when she's sleeping. She'll be sorry she let this happen to me. As we are leaving, I see the cat come out with its person. Its side is shaved and there's a bigger poke than I have on my side. That's my only consolation. Looks like the cat got it worse than me.

19

We're at her house, she gives me more treats. I'm sore. That wasn't nice of her. Of course, I take the treats. Then I walk over, almost limping, to my bed and lay down. She said she was sorry, but I don't care. The farmer never did anything like this to me. He gave me a pill once and I pooped a lot, some stringy things came out, but it didn't hurt like this did. Where is my farmer?

Time has gone by. I don't have the concept of time down exactly, but I have learned its framing. Days have passed and they have become months. I have learned a few things through the passing of time. Long legs is my new mother. I understand now that the bigger dog at the farm was my mother. Long legs may not have given birth to me, but she has become the person who takes care of me and makes sure I eat, bathe, and she helps me get well when I need to and plays with me. This place is my home now. I am never going back to the farm and although I miss the farm so much, I will survive here. She seems motivated to love me by the very actions she initiates.

We go for walks. This is different from me walking around at the farm. At the farm, I was free. Here, I am no longer free to walk where I please or as long as I please. The decisions I was once able to make for myself she now makes for me. Who decided that... not me. I don't know why; she just seems to have more power than me. I don't know how she knows what I want or need but she gets it right *most* of the time. The times that she doesn't, well, I'm learning to let her know when she has failed me. Her name is now mom. This, her home, is now my home, and that older lady is my gramma. She really loves me. She brings gifts and just really loves me. I'm not sure what my life would have been at the farm if she had never taken me from there. I think I'm gonna be okay though. I think this life will be good.

My gramma says my ears are like velvet. She is always smelling me and rubbing my ears across her face. She's too much sometimes but she sure does love me. I am becoming very cute, so I'm told. My soft hair is multicolored, and my nose is always cold. I have lots of patches on me and I don't look like any other dog I have seen since I've been here. I am truly one of the prettiest puppies that has ever been born... at least that's what my gramma says all the time.

Look at me in the next picture, waiting at the door for my mom to come out. I'm sweet enough to be a toothache. She's trying to rest... too bad for her, I want to play.

I may be the sweetest thing you've ever seen.

I'm ready for the next chapter of my life. I think it will be good from here out. I don't know today, but I will soon learn that there will be a vast array of things that will happen in my life. Good, bad, and everything in between. They say life is what you make it, I say it will be what my wonderful mother makes it, and she will make it great for me. It will cost her, but she will give me an awesome life.

Chapter 2

THE EARLY YEARS
Ah, youth.

I didn't do anything… really, I didn't.

There have been a lot of changes over the last few months. Let me give you a review of what's happening in this next stage of my life. First, I must tell you about my Grandpa's Pines and his cabin up north. They are the next best thing to being on the farm. The Pines – this is the name of his home. It's twenty acres of pines that my grandpa lives on. Mom and I will live there at one point in our lives. I'm still young, but this is the best place in the world – until I discover the cabin. Then my gramma takes me to the beach! We live near the beach... wow... the beach! There is no life better than mine. Let's start with where we live.

My mom and I live in town. It's a town right on the shores of Lake Michigan. It's cool, there's lots of people here. Most are nice but my mom talks about how some people have too much money, not us. From the looks of some of the dogs I see... she's right. We live in an apartment, we've moved a couple of times, but I like it here. I get to go outside. I have to go on a chain. What a stupid idea that is. Who's the idiot that invented the dog chain? I'd like to meet that person. I would bite them so hard! I would put that chain on them all day long. I can run, but I can't leave the yard, and I can't chase the squirrels. What is life for if you can't chase squirrels? I have to be on a chain when we walk downtown too. How can I run up to people and beg for food if I have to be on a chain all the time? Seriously, this chain thing is abuse. It's abuse and somebody should do something about it... they won't. Apparently, I have proven that if I am let off the chain I

24

will run away. I don't really call it running away. I call it wandering, wondering, wanderlust. I guess the fact that mom and gramma have had to *find* me a few times, made them decide that I must be restrained. It's bull! I'm gonna start a movement. Oh wait… there's a squirrel… get ready mom… here we go!

Is anybody going to let me in – please let me in.

I go to my gramma's all the time. We visit, and sometimes I stay with her. She is the nicest person in the world. She loves me so much. I am her *only* granddog. She doesn't have any human grand babies, so, I'm it. We go for walks, and she gets me treats. The one thing my gramma does that is beyond awesome is, she takes me to the beach.

You would not believe this beach. It goes on forever. There are a couple of piers and some kind of nets that people throw balls back and forth at with other people. We don't. We walk on the beach. Gramma wants me to walk in the water. This lake is unending. There's nothing out there but lake. I'm not going in it. What if it washes me out? I may never come back. People play in it all day long. They must get so tired. There are big people, little people and I just saw a lady lay a small person on its back in the water. She must want it to float away, that's mean. She's holding it but it could float away on these big waves. They must be at least six inches high. I'm not going out there. I'm not taking any chances.

There are people on surfboards out there, standing. I don't think anyone has told them how dangerous it is out there. I'm not going near it. That big water will probably swallow them soon, I could've told them, too bad for them. There are boats of all kinds out there. I'm not getting on any.

I will, however, run in circles on this beach forever! I just run around in circles in the sand. I run, and I run, and I run. I don't dig, I don't chase anything, I just run in the sand. It's so cool. My feet dig in and there I go. Gramma holds my leash and I go round and round. When I get tired, we stop and rest. Then, before you know it, I am running again. The sand in my feet, the sun on my body, the wind in my face. It's the next best thing to hanging your head out the car window, which is pretty cool, and I do it as often as I can. Ears flowing in the breeze and the soft wind comes across my eyes and nose. I open my mouth and swallow that wind, as much of it as I can. It's mine to take in. An occasional bug may make it down my throat, but that's okay. I'm a dog, I lick myself, what's a bug here and there.

I love the beach. My gramma does too. She likes to sit and watch the lake. I let her sometimes but then I remind her why we're here… so I can run in the sand. She watches as big and small boats come and go and people play in the water. Birds fly by and the sun sets in the distance. She really loves the lake. She never goes in the water; she just watches the lake. Me, I run in circles again and again in the sand. All in all, we are both very happy at the beach. We stay as long as we can and then we come back another day and another and another. I can't get enough of the beach. It will become a place in my life where I spend a lot of time. I will love it all my life and I will miss it when we leave… and we will.

Today is my birthday, at least that's what mom and gramma are talking about. We go for a walk downtown and then we stop at this place on the boardwalk. Gramma holds my leash as mom walks up to the counter. She comes back with something in her hand and bends over to offer it to me. I look at it… I take a lick… it's awesome… it's ice cream… ice cream… ice cream is great! For the next twelve years or so we will go for ice cream on my birthday with gramma, every year. What a memory. This life just keeps getting better.

I eat all my ice cream and we go for a walk out on the pier, that's next to the beach, so… you guessed it… I run in circles on the beach as the two of them stand there and smile. I make them smile a lot. They love me more than anything in the world, both of them, and truth be told, I love them too. They are my new family.

My grandparents don't live together. They like each other, and they're nice to each other, they just don't live together, go figure. My grandpa lives a long way from us. It's at least an hour and a half in the car, that's a long ride for a dog. Now we've talked about this before, I don't know exactly how I know language and things, but I do. I guess I am a genius dog, that's all I can figure, cuz' I know a lot of stuff. I think I am probably smarter than most dogs, but that's just what I think.

Anyhow, I have to tell you about The Pines. That's where my grandpa lives, and it is awesome. It's twenty acres of huge, tall, pine trees. It's the most wonderful place. I don't have to be on a chain when I'm there. Either they trust me here or they don't care if I run away, but I won't, I love it here. There are rabbits, mice, squirrels... so many squirrels in the trees. It would take me years to count all the trees here. There's a big yard that we play in, and grandpa has a nice place for us to stay.

We stay with him a lot. He's a really nice guy. He has dogs of his own, so he doesn't spoil me quite like my gramma does. That's okay, she makes up for everybody else. There's a farm just down the road. That's where my grandpa's mom and dad live. They live together, weird! They're very nice people and they really, really, like my mom. They're very nice to her. They have tons of land here, with trees, a stream, hills, meadows, these people just have it all. They also have a big barn and silos and *so* much room to run. I think that's what I like the most over here is that I don't have to be on my leash. There's no beach but there's freedom for a while. It's the best of both worlds and the best of all people. Everyone loves me, they just love me.

I have gotten into some trouble here and there. You'll hear about that a little later. I can't be perfect. I must be close though cuz' nobody yells, and they are always giving me treats, always. They must have a lot of money... ha-ha.

So, when we come to grandpa's I get to run. I love to run. I get to play in the dirt and mud. I get to run through the woods and the grasses at the grandparents' farm, and the blueberry patch. A dog should always have a place to run. You won't believe how many different animals are here in these pines and the woods across the road. Of course, there are squirrels, there are squirrels everywhere. God made squirrels for dogs. There are birds, I can't reach them, but if I could...

There are deer. They're strange animals. They're pretty but they don't like to play with dogs. I have seen them run through The Pines and through the woods and fields across the road. Then I have seen them hanging in my grandpa's yard... dead. Yes, I said dead! I guess they shouldn't have run through his yard. I think there's more to it than that. I have seen him dress up in his *hunting gear* he calls it. He leaves and comes back with dead deer, fox, rabbits, birds, and fish. Oh, and squirrels. I'm good with the squirrels, they irritate everybody. I don't know what the other things did to him.

My mom and my uncle Zack have gone with him too and both have come back with dead animals. I hope I never make them so mad that they kill me. I hear them talk about hunting, whatever that is. It seems to be the thing that kills all the animals. Hunting.

Over the years I learned that hunting is normal for many people who believe in the sport. They always eat what they kill so I cannot fault them. My grandpa has killed racoons that were sick in our yard. I guess there's a place for everything under the sun. I can understand a little. I'm a hunter too and those squirrels better keep their distance, or they will see what hunting can do! Just being honest.

The best thing about The Pines is *the pines*, the *trees* are so tall and so beautiful. The wind rushes through them and I just stand and let it move my ears past my face. The air is warm, the sun is bright, the grass is coarse, I love this yard in The Pines. My grandpa is about the kindest man I know. Now, I don't know a lot of people but he sure is at the top of my list. He works hard and he's nice. I couldn't ask for anything more, until he takes me to the cabin!

The cabin... what a place, the cabin. I know it's way up north cuz it's another hour and a half drive in the car. We usually ride up with grandpa. He's a quiet man so I can sleep a lot on the way up. We get there and mom opens the door and I jump out and just stand for a moment gazing out at this magnificent piece of heaven on the top of the hill with pine trees surrounding it to the point that you can't see the road below. The only thing I see is a small cut out yard and the one room cabin we'll be staying in.

This place is in the middle of nowhere, a dog's dream. Nothing but land to run on and the wildlife up here is way different than at The Pines. There are deer here and grandpa hunts them, and there's turkey here that he hunts too. It's not fair that he can hunt things but if I bring a dead animal to the door... I get in trouble. It's just not fair. I'm just being a hunter gatherer, kind of, sort of, well, maybe not, just a hunter. There are porcupines, beavers, wolves, bears, bobcats, hawks, weasels, foxes, and more. Some of these may have been at The Pines, but not like here. It can be a little dangerous at night to roam around here, but they let me. They keep good track of me though. They do care about me after all... they do.

We don't do much when we're here, just hang out. My mom's uncle comes down to visit sometimes and a few others here and there. My grandpa loves it here. It's pretty basic and there's not a lot of conveniences like there are at home or at grammas, but we get by. I roam the land and make sure no unwanted dogs or cats are around. I may find a dead animal here and there and if I bring it back nobody appreciates my effort. They throw it away and I usually have to get a bath. Why, I'm not the dirty one. I like to lay in the driveway in the sun or on the cold cabin floor.

This cabin has been in grandpa's family for over seventy years, I think. His grandpa and his dad and a few other people planted every one of these pine trees on this hill. Every single one of them. People don't do that kind of thing anymore. Nobody wants to work for it, they just want to have it. My grandpa isn't like that, he's a man who will work hard for what he wants, and he will enjoy it hard too. He's a great man in my view.

We usually stay here for a weekend. There is electricity, but no running water, no air conditioning, no cozy bed like mine at home. A one room cabin where everyone who comes stays. If someone snores, like me, everyone is within ear shot. My mom likes to sleep in, but my grandpa doesn't. Grandpa wins most of the time. I wake early too and the first thing me and grandpa need to do is go outside and pee. It's that rustic here that right out the door is usually the best place to pee. It's amazing how happy and content people can be when they just sit around for the day and relax and do a few things and then rest again. No cable, that's okay.

They go to eat a lot and make me stay here alone. I don't like it, but I have no say. I am not one of those dogs that will destroy everything in their sight if you leave them alone, but I can get my point across if I need to. I can nap, run, play, eat and pretty much do whatever I want up here. It's amazing how many hours I can just get lost in these woods. I know my boundaries pretty well and I don't stray too far away. If anything comes after me, I run as fast as I can, and mom opens the door and I fly into where my safety is.

I get a lot of scrapes up here. Not like at home. Usually, I am the only dog here, no cats allowed, or at least there have never been any here. Occasionally someone will bring their dog, but I make sure they know this is my domain. Grandpa has had dogs over the years, and they come, and I let them think that they are in charge, but they're not. This is my haven, and I will protect it to the end. I'm not bad with other dogs but I'm not around many and sometimes when I am they bother me. I just ignore their irritating attitudes. Grandpa's dogs are always bigger than me. I don't care, they get locked in cages all the time, not me. I am free no matter where I am, here, at grandpa's, at gramma's, at home. Well, when I'm inside at home and at gramma's, it's when we go outside that I have to be on that stupid leash and chain. I hate that leash, but I know it's not going anywhere anytime soon. Well, at least not in town and that's why I love it at The Pines and the cabin. So much... freedom... sweet freedom.

It's Sunday morning and we are heading back to grandpas. He likes to leave early Sunday morning to avoid the traffic. He still has the whole day left but he likes to leave early. That's okay cuz I get to run in the woods there too. I'm a happy camper. I get to run around for a couple of hours before we leave, check out all my favorite spots and then take a nice long nap all the way home. Life couldn't be better.

The Life & Times of Dave's Saving Grace

We're back at home now and something is happening this morning that is different from every other day. Mom is taking some of my toys when she leaves for work, now she's taking me. What's going on? We go for a short ride. I'm up for a ride, but this is different. Something weird is happening. We're at a place that has a bunch of dogs. All kinds, big ones, small ones, scary looking ones. What is this? My mom is talking to a couple of people. They're all looking at me. What... what did I do?

She's signing something. She hands one of the people something, picks up her purse, and heads for the door. Not without me you're not. I start to follow her as tears come to her eyes. Suddenly, I am stopped dead in my tracks. One of those people has my leash in their hand. Whoa, whoa, whoa there. Let go of me. She won't. I look and my mom is out the door and getting in her car. She forgot to take me. I start howling to let her know. She drives away... without me! I start to cry as my mom is gone from my sight. Those people try to be nice and tell me that I am staying here until my mom comes back. I haven't been with anyone but my mom or my gramma since I left the farm.

She's given me away. I am so sad. I could never imagine I could be this sad. My mom has left me, she's given me away, she's gone. My heart is broken. I don't wanna be here, I wanna go home. What will I do? They try to make me happy and get me to play with other dogs, but I can't, I am distraught. I keep looking around and there are many people and dogs here, but not my mom. She left me, I thought she loved me. She said she loved me. Why didn't she just give me to my gramma, she would take me, she loves me.

The day goes by slowly, but it goes by, and the other dogs seem to be happy, and they play together and then a really nice dog comes over and offers me their toy. I look at them and take the toy. I have a friend. Someone comes through the door and my friend gets really excited. Before I know it, he's leaving with the person. He doesn't even fight it. He walks right out with them as happy as can be.

Then one by one the other dogs leave with people too. What is happening here? My mother abandoned me, and these guys are going away with people that they seem to love. Then, without notice the door opens, I hear my mom's voice calling to me. I turn around and there she is. She's come back. I start screaming as I run to her and just scream and scream. She holds me and tries to calm me down, but I can't. I am just so thankful that she came back for me.

They gather my things and hand them to her and she takes my leash. We walk out the door, and in the car, she tries to make small talk. Asking me how my day was and telling me about hers. How dare she! I made it clear by looking out the window and ignoring her all the way home that I wasn't happy that she abandoned me for the whole day.

At home she gives me food and fresh water. I am not talking to her yet. She tries very hard to be nice. Then she pulls out a new toy and gives it to me. I still ignore her, but I take that toy and I play with it hard. By bedtime I'm over her abandonment and I take my place right beside her in bed and we fall asleep as if everything was perfect again, because it is.

The next morning starts out the same. She grabs some of my toys and takes me to the car. The drive is the same and we pull up to the same place as yesterday. Same routine, she's in, she's out, and I have to stay. About another week of this and I get the routine. I even start to play with some of the other dogs. I stay away from a few because they look mean, and I don't like mean dogs or mean people. No thanks. The people are mostly nice and most of the dogs are too. There are a couple dogs that are bullies. I'm not naming breeds, but some are just mean, and I think they have been all their lives, you can just tell.

For whatever reason, I have come to understand that this is our new normal. I stay with her at night and here all day. It seems my mom needs some time away from me each day and then she comes and gets me at night, and we go home, and everything is great. The next day we start all over again. As long as I can keep Rufus off my tail, I'll be okay. He gets punished here a lot. A real snippy dude.

Today is different though, my gramma has come for me. She is so excited to see me, we leave, and she takes me to the beach. Remember how much I love the beach. I get to run around in circles in the sand and run and run. Gosh I love to run. She watches the waves and me as I get all my energy out. After a while, I'm tired and so we just sit on the sand and watch the water as it goes nowhere. I love my gramma. We go to her house, and I get to spend the night. I love to come here; she always does nice things for me. She has new toys for me and always has treats. The next day my mom comes and picks me up and we spend the day together. The whole daycare thing has become routine. I heard her talking to gramma and it looks like I'll be going there five days a week and then spend weekends with her.

It's the weekend, it's a great day. She rubs my ears and I snuggle up to her. Sometimes I need to move her hand with my nose because she forgets to pet me constantly. I like her to pet me all the time. She's good about it, for the most part.

It's time for me to go to sleep now. She doesn't tell me that, I know when I'm tired. I sleep in the dark and sometimes she still has the TV on. I pull the covers over my head, my nighttime routine. She knows that when the blankets over me, it's time for bed. She's pretty good about being quiet then. After all, a girl needs her sleep. As you can see it doesn't matter where I am, I need my blanket to sleep. Traveling down the road, in bed, in the living room, at gramma's, at The Pines, or at the cabin, as long as I have my blanket, sleep is right around the corner.

There is comfort under the blanket.

Life goes on. We go see gramma, take walks, get ice cream, hang out, go to The Pines, and the cabin. My mom and I take long drives together too. I love to hang my head out the window and let my ears fly in the wind. The wind is so nice across my forehead. She loves to see new places, so we just drive and drive. Sometimes she goes out at night but that's okay cuz' I guard the house until she comes home. She's young, she needs to get away every now and then.

I like where we live, what we do, who we are. Long legs turned out to be the best thing that could ever happen to me. She is kind and caring and she loves me and does a lot of things that only a mother could do. Then again, she is my mother and I love her so much. If she's ever sad, once in a while, I'll kiss her face and let her pet me so that she will feel better. Petting me always makes everyone feel better, especially me.

I became used to the daycare routine, the other dogs, our weekends together, and going to all the places we go. Today though, there's something else going on here. She's packing her suitcase... with way more stuff than when we need to go to grandpa's or the cabin. She never stays with gramma, just me. So, what's up here? She's taking all sorts of stuff and she's packing my stuff too. Well, wherever we're going, which must be a long way away, we're going together so I'm okay with it.

Gramma just walked in so she must be going with us. They each grab some of the bags and carry them out to gramma's car. Oh, we must be going with her. We all get in and I'm hanging my head out the window wondering where the road is taking us. It must be really far away. Then, only after a little while, we pull into a drive, stop, and mom gets my stuff and me out. My leash is on, and we head for a house. I turn to look, and gramma is still in her car. Come on I think, we all have to go, together.

We walk around to the basement and a lady opens the door. We walk in… what in the heck is going on here? There are cages everywhere… why are there cages everywhere… what are the cages everywhere for? They talk, she sets my stuff down, I head for the door. I'm not staying here. She can, but I'm going with gramma. No, I'm not, she is. I'm staying here. Why did she bring so much stuff for one day? Must be a new daycare.

They talk for quite a while and mom gives this lady her number and says she'll see her soon. Soon? Soon is now, right? She hands my leash to this lady and turns toward the door. She looks back at me and I am just staring, waiting for her to take my leash again, get my stuff, and get on our way with gramma.

That's not what happened, not at all. She bends down and kisses me… a long kiss. She walks to the door, and I try to follow but the lady holding my leash won't let me. My mom walks out the door and I am horrified. I begin to cry and howl, and the lady pulls on my leash and pushes me into a cage and walks out of the room. She shuts the lights off and it's dark. I'm in panic mode because no one treats me this way.

Days go by and I mean days. It must have been hundreds of days since my mom left me here. I guess this is my life now. I do get to come out of the cage during the day most of the time. The cage though is where I am forced to sleep and where I am whenever this lady feels like putting me in there, and it's been a lot. Other dogs have come and gone, and some are still here. I don't have my blanket with me, so sleeping is very hard. I am sad most of the time.

I've lost track of time. I think it's been a few months now and I have succumbed to the pain that is now my life. I don't know how much life I have left, but it's going to be very sad from here on out.

The lady comes down and lets me out of the cage. Why? The other dogs are still in their cages. I feel bad for them. Then, the door opens, and my mom walks in! I start yelping and screaming and she rushes up to me and bends over and hugs me. She keeps hugging me and kissing me. After all these years she has come back for me. She begins to gather my stuff and the lady says to her. "How was your week in Florida?" Week? I've been here for months... but if they want to say it was a week that's fine. My mom is here, and I am going home with her. That's all that matters now.

When we get home, mom unpacks, and I find my blanket and she gives me a new toy. She unpacks her stuff and mine and I play. Well actually, I rip out the stuffing of my new toy. When she is done and we're ready to rest, I crawl under my blanket, and she puts her hand on my head and rubs it softly. She kisses me and hugs me and says she missed me so much. Then why did you leave me for so long? I'm telling you that week felt like months. But all is well now, and our lives are perfect. At least for a minute. Sadly, this will happen again when she goes on another vacation.

I've spoken about my blanket a couple of times. I have never been a dog that needs to be told to go to bed or needs to be put in bed. I have always known when I am tired. I don't like the light of the TV, a lamp light, the outdoor light, or anything to interrupt my nap or sleep. So, what I did as a young pup was to pull a blanket over my head. Now I can just shoot my mom a look and she'll get a blanket and put it over me, and I fall asleep. Anyone who knows me knows that if there is a blanket over my head, leave me alone! I am resting… do not disturb.

Sometimes when we're at grandmas and the two of them are talking, they're always talking, I hide under the blanket. These two never shut up when they're around each other. At least at grandpa's it's quiet. He doesn't have a lot to say and usually just likes to hang out. Not my mom and gramma. Talk, talk, talk, always talking, unless they're watching a movie, then it's just some talking, but there's still plenty of talking about the movie. If I need a nap or they're talking forever, here comes the blanket. I like dark spaces where I know I'm safe. I'll hang out under that blanket until I'm ready to play, eat, or go outside.

Those blankets though, as you can see in the pictures, have become a part of my life. They will always give me comfort until my life ends… ugh. More about that later.

Blankets... a good thing.

One thing I remember about my youth that changed over time, was the way people would approach me. As a puppy, I was always greeted with love and baby talk, always. People would hold my chin, scratch my back, and kiss my face. They would cuddle with me and pet me over and over when I was a puppy. As I grew to a young dog, it changed just a little. Now they would pet me and pat my head. They were kind to me but the rush of love that once covered me was gone. I rarely got in any trouble as a puppy. I was cute. As a youngster I became pretty, but pretty is treated differently than cute. Pretty is responsible when you have an accident in the house, when you bring in a stick with bugs on it, or when you run off for a moment. Pretty is still loved, it's just expected to be responsible. I am not a responsible dog, that's what I have a mother for.

Then comes age, later years, old age, senior doghood, call it what you want... age will come to me. Senior dogs are treated much like senior people, with a misguided understanding that we are unable to hear, walk, run, hold our pee, or see. That's not who I am at this time. I may be getting there, but I'm not there yet. That is way past old age. I am going to be vital until the last day of my life. I think I am I hope I am. I guess we'll see. I would hope I could live forever, or at least as long as my mom so she won't be sad when I die... but she will, sadly she will.

The Life & Times of Dave's Saving Grace

Chapter 3

THERE WERE BUMPS ALONG THE WAY
Ouch!

Make up your mind… which way?

    I remember soon after I came to live with long legs, mom, a terrible thing happened to me. Being born on the farm can leave you open to some pretty rough conditions. She realized within a few weeks that I had mites. Now it was up to her to get rid of them and do it as fast as she could. Mites can be horrible, and I was just over six weeks old. I was itching and scratching and in pain and she could see it. Lucky me, we got to go to the vet again. I don't like the vet, he's always sticking his fingers somewhere, poking me, or grabbing my throat. When I get older, I'm gonna bite him right in the hand. Later in life I'll hear my gramma talk about how her new, young granddaughter bit her dentist when he stuck his finger in her mouth and she didn't like it. Good job girl! Anyhow, back to the mites.

They were everywhere on me. I could hardly move. The vet gave mom some stuff to wash me in. I think it was lye… yep, it was lye. She had to put Vaseline on my eyes so the lye wouldn't burn them. Then, she filled the tub, put that lye liquid in it and picked me up off the floor and dunked me in the tub. SHE DUNKED ME IN A VAT OF LYE… A VAT OF LYE!! Well, it was actually the tub, felt like a vat. I hope this works because this stuff is horrible. It burns, it hurts, and the mites are digging into me like crazy.

I remember she took me out of the tub, cleaned my eyes out and rubbed my wet coat with a towel. Then she had the nerve to look at me and kiss my face. Drop dead lady. Let me put you in a vat of lye and see how you like it. She tried to be nice to me, but I wasn't having it. Well, I guess if I'm being honest, I'm a dog, treats, kisses, playing with my toys, going outside, those are kinda my thing. I did my best to be mad at her for what she had done to me, and I think I did pretty good. The anger lasted at least ten or fifteen minutes. But I think she knew better then to ever do that to me again. Apparently, she didn't.

Within a week or so she had to do it again. The mites had survived and if she didn't get rid of them, I might not survive. Mites are dangerous, they hurt and they're relentless in their need for puppy blood. Please don't let your dog suffer. Truth be told, long legs was very worried and doing her best to get them off me. I think it hurt her as much to do the treatment, as it did for me to get it. Wait a minute... no... I don't think that's right. I never saw her cry or scratch until she was bleeding... yeah... it didn't hurt her as much as it did me. She did her best to make it better, and after the second drop in the tub, they were gone forever. Now, don't confuse this with torture. It was done with love, concern, and all the kindness she could muster. It had to be done, it just wasn't a good experience. I would visit bad experiences again in my life, not with mites though.

And then there was the time they poisoned me... see... I told you. You think I'm kidding but my gramma had to call poison control to see if I was going to die! And yet, I wasn't the first dog they had poisoned. I remember hearing them talk to others about the other dog. I couldn't believe it. What kind of monsters are these two people? Well, they really aren't, not at all. Here's the first story.

My mom didn't have any dogs of her own before me, but my gramma... she had lots over the years, and I mean lots. They had a little thing, a Yorkie, when my mom and my uncle were young and lived with gramma. They talk about her like she's a princess. You'll see a picture of her later and although she's really cute and sweet as a pea... as cute as me? I don't think so. But I digress, Lillie was the smallest dog they had ever owned. My gramma likes big dogs, Bouvier Des Flandres, Irish Setters, Chesapeake Bay Retrievers, and other large breeds.

Lillie was a dog though that they all loved. They got her when she was a puppy, and she could never get more than seven or eight pounds on her. She was the kind of dog (from the way they talk), that was just awesome. My mom has pictures of Lillie with her. They just loved that dog, yet my gramma poisoned her.

She, my gramma, was painting a bedroom in their house. Now this is something you should know about my gramma. We could walk in her house one day and it would be so cute. The next day we go there, every wall is painted a different color and the furniture is moved completely around in the room. I can't find my toys and I don't know where my bed went. This happened all the time, for years. I'm telling you this, so you understand she was at it again, painting.

She had a friend helping her and they were painting the small bedroom in the house. Lillie, that little princess, came in and she scurried her out of the room. About an hour later my mom, who was in her early teens they said, came flying in the house screaming at my gramma. Lillie, (in my view), was trying to get attention, at first. She was walking around the yard and falling down.

Gramma ran out, and there she was, falling down, over and over again. My mom, her brother, and my gramma took her to the vet. They said she kept passing out in the car. What a drama queen! Well, that's what I would think if the next thing hadn't happened. At the vet, after a while, they found out that Lillie had walked through the paint drop cloth that had some paint on it, and she had ingested the paint through her feet and had been poisoned. Oh my gosh! Poisoned? Just by walking through something? Yep, she sure was. She almost died and they talk about how sad and scared they were when this happened to her. She had to stay at the vets for nine days and it cost my gramma a thousand dollars. There are many stories about other dogs that my gramma has spent a boatload of money on, even when she didn't have one... me. Maybe someday she'll tell those stories too.

They finally brought her home and they learned a very expensive lesson. Don't worry though, there's way more lessons that they will learn about owning pets as the years go by.

So on with my story. We all lived together, me, my mom, and my gramma. Saving money or something I recall. Anyhow, I don't exactly remember why, I think I was very itchy, I think that was it. They decided to give me some Benadryl for the itching. That was something that could help me calm down at times and let me rest. That's not what happened this time. I started getting very drowsy.

I started to drop over and try to stand up and drop over. Well, after a while, they thought something was wrong.

They didn't know what to do but I was going downhill quickly. My mom was really worried and scared and so my gramma called poison control. You know, the place you call when your kids eat the laundry soap pods. They don't usually have people call who poison their pets and they really didn't mean to do it, but that's what they did. They poisoned me. Of course, first, they Googled it – how to stop a dog's itch. Google gave them the protocol to follow, and they did… they thought they did… they didn't. They were supposed to give me five teaspoons of Benadryl. You know, to calm me down and stop me from itching. Well, I calmed down alright. I was almost comatose. They gave me five *tablespoons*. Teaspoon, tablespoon, close? No, not really. It was four times more than I should have had, after all, I weigh less than forty pounds. That's a lot and my system didn't know what to do so instead of calming me down… it was knocking me out. Now, I'm not sure that it would have killed me, but they sure freaked out. I have never had so much water and they had to keep me awake. I didn't want to be awake, but I was. They walked me, they played with me, they talked to me. On and on and on. I didn't think it was ever going to stop.

Finally, after hours of attention, water, walking and just getting in my face, they let me rest, and rest I did. I slept for a long time. They woke me up almost every half hour, so it wasn't great sleep, but it was finally over. They never meant to do it, just a misunderstanding. I think the lesson they learned that day was to read the advice very well and to make sure you know what you're doing. What had I learned that day? These two people would do anything it took to keep me safe and save me from anything. That I knew for sure now. I knew these two people would never do anything to hurt me again, and I knew they would always do anything to save me if I needed it, and I would. I forgave them, and of course there were many treats involved in their redemption for that occurrence.

That wasn't the last time they would need to step in to save me. My mom and I were living a quiet life in our little beach town. We had a nice apartment and I got to go outside all the time and rest in the front yard. My mom hates to clean up dog poop, I hate to tell you all, there is poop with a dog. Can't be avoided. So, I was outside watching the birds in the trees and finishing my business when I noticed a big dog coming down the street. When I say big, I mean *big*, it was a Rottweiler. I am no more than a thirty-to-forty-pound beagle. I'm not gonna get any bigger but that dog got bigger with each step toward me. I barked a time or two at him as he came down the sidewalk, on a leash, being held by his owner who was riding a bike. What could go wrong, right? Just everything. As he approached me, I moved a little closer to the house. This dog was huge!

Then, out of nowhere, he came after me. I tried to

run, but I was on a chain and there was nowhere for me to go. The lady fell off the bike and the Rottweiler came toward me with an unearned vendetta. As I tried to move away, he laid his mouth into my side. Ripped me wide open. I was screaming and he continued to attack me. His owner stood up and tried to get him off me, but he wasn't going anywhere. My mom came running out. A lot of screaming ensued by both women and the lady finally got her dog off me.

These two lived above us. She apologized for the attack and pulled her dog away and went upstairs. That's it?! That was it. My mom was scared and didn't know what to do. I was bleeding all over and my side was torn open, and I was in shock. She called my gramma and of course she flew over to the house, and they took me to the vet. Great, my favorite place on earth.

We had to wait because it was after hours, so I just kept bleeding, and we kept waiting. The vet finally came, and of course more pain was just around the corner for me. There were shots, stitches, some ointment, some drugs, and a razor involved in the fix. I'm tired and now the drugs are kicking in. We go home and I am going to rest for a long time. It's over… nope, not at all.

Next comes the lesson and the money. My mom isn't rich, so my gramma paid the bill. Like I said before, they would do anything for me, and they did. My mom didn't want any trouble and was okay with just letting it go. My gramma on the other hand, isn't easy to push around.

She thought that me, on a chain, in my own yard, with no way to reach the sidewalk, could in no way end in me being attacked and her paying for it.

My mom called the girl upstairs and told her how much it cost to close the wound that her dog had inflicted on my side and expected her to be accountable. Okay, now we wait for her to take responsibility for her dog's unprovoked attack. That's not quite what happened. As we waited for her to come down and take care of the vet bill… she didn't. Instead, her brother came down. I was laying on the couch, almost asleep, those drugs were pretty good. He announced to my mom and my gramma that his sister would not be paying for anything. It was my fault, me, the beagle. I am the one who lunged at her dog and caused him to react. I am a thirty-five -pound beagle, (give or take a few pounds) he's a one-hundred-pound Rottweiler, you do the math. If I had lunged at him, he would have taken me out with a snap of my neck. I'm not sure that wasn't his plan to start with before his owner pulled as hard as she could to get him away from me.

Anyhow, this guy, Mr. Big Stuff, Mr. Tough Guy was just letting these two women know how it was going to be. How things would go down. Immediately I felt sorry for him. What a fool! My gramma, good or bad, doesn't respond well to "anyone" telling her what to do and how things are going to be. She's always quite aware of exactly what the situation is. So, she shared a little truth with him. The bully just stood there like he was the king in the room.

I'm pretty sure his chest was a little puffed out, just for a moment though, only a moment.

As I said, my gramma doesn't back down easily, and has no interest in being put in a corner. She shared with him that she had already called one of her personal friends at the police department and they were on their way to take a police report. She would then call her insurance company and report the dog and finally would be more than happy to call the humane society to have this dog picked up. Who knows from there what could happen to him. Shall I say he was at the least, stunned. He was. He really didn't know what to do, and amid his foot in his mouth posture, the police showed up.

They assured him that everything my gramma had said would come to fruition if he wanted to press the matter, or his sister refused to take responsibility for her dog's actions. Well, this guy's tune changed in a breath. He begged my mom for grace, saying that his sister couldn't afford the bill. Although my gramma has a backbone of steel, my mom didn't. She has a heart of gold. She pleaded with her mother to only make her pay half the bill. My gramma agreed and it was taken care of. It's over... nope not at all.

The situation seemed to be taken care of and I healed. I was left with a scar for the rest of my life, but it healed. I was also left with a fear of attack anytime another dog came at me quickly. The girl upstairs and her dog moved soon after. So, the bully was gone from the neighborhood. Yet, that wasn't the end, there was more to the story. Sometime later, my gramma found out that the Rottweiler, before he attacked me, had bitten a child. Apparently, it was a young child and there was no permanent damage, and she (or her bully brother) was able to talk the person out of calling the police or reporting the incident.

The lesson here, stand up for yourself and your pets. Don't let some bully stop you from reporting something that could either cause further damage or be an incident that the perpetrator (the Rottweiler) could do again. This dog should have been put down. He had too much power in his mouth with a history of bad behavior that should not have gone unnoticed. In their defense, my mom and her mother didn't know the history of the dog at that time. Not in their defense, they should have paid more attention to what actually happened and how it could affect someone, human or not, in the future. I know they both pray that this dog didn't hurt anyone else, dog, cat, or human, but if he did, they missed their opportunity to stop it. Pay attention to your pets needs and deeds and make sure they are all safe and responsible for their actions, good or bad.

I never got in a lot of trouble, but there was a little along the way. It was just me and mom, what could happen? Things did and I found myself in hot water more than once. House training was a challenge for both of us, but we lived through it and came out good on the other side. What else could happen… well.

There was one time I remember getting into trouble and it really was my fault. That's what my mom said. I was never around a lot of other dogs. My mother did have this one friend though that had a little dog. I didn't really like that little dog. She was spoiled and thought she had the run of the place wherever she went. That's a problem for me. My home is my home… and my gramma's home… that's mine too.

We were at my gramma's one night when they came over. My gramma's house is my domain, no one else's. End of story. As usual though, this little thing came in and immediately snipped at me. Well, I made my intentions very clear. I wouldn't bite her because I knew I would get in big trouble for that. So, what I did was genius, I thought. I body slammed her against the wall. You heard me right. I took my hips and I swung them right into her side, knocking her off her feet immediately. Just like you're imagining. Wham! Right up against the wall and to the floor. I was just warning her, what's the big deal? I got yelled at and they all swooned over that little b…., you know what I mean. She was trying to weasel in on my gramma… not gonna happen. Yet, I'm the one who was scolded, fine.

I walked into the living room, jumped on the arm of the couch, and stared at the wall for the next hour or so. My mom tried to talk sweet to me, but I wasn't having it. I ignored all of them and would continue to sulk until the little brat was gone. I let the two of them, mom, and gramma, know exactly how I felt about it. I don't think I was very nice to my mom or gramma for the rest of the night. But then there was a new day and treats, oh how I love those treats. I guess I've punished them enough and not taking the treat would be punishment to me and I couldn't have that. Once again, all is well.

Now these were by far the worst things that happened to me in my life. The other thing that caused some real concern was a situation of my own making. Do you know how bad coke is for you? Sure, you do, but do you stop drinking it... no. My gramma doesn't either, but that was me with sticks. I love to eat sticks, but they don't come out well. I spent a lot of time outside in my youth. The Pines, the cabin, the beach, the park, and the yard. You know what all these places have in common? Sticks. Yep, sticks. I love sticks, playing with them, catching them, and eating them. I chew well, I really do. The problem is that sticks don't come out as easy as they go in.

Just a fun little hobby will turn into a real medical disadvantage throughout my lifetime. I will visit the vet more than a few times because of sticks in my stomach that didn't digest well. My mom does her best to keep me from eating them, but it won't stop me. I spend a lot of time on my own in some of the places we go, and there's no one there to stop me from eating the sticks.

Later in my life, this will become a real problem as the doctor needs to prescribe things to help me. There will even be physical interference by the doctor into my bowels, you don't even wanna know. I wish I could have stopped, but I didn't. The fun that I had all that time in eating those stupid sticks... well, that became the horror I had to live with, in problems with digestion, bowel movements, and pain later in life.

It wasn't just me though who went through some hard times. My mom, throughout my time with her, lost family and friends and others. I always did my best to keep her mind off the hard times. I would know, just know when she needed me to give her a kiss, go for a walk, rest, hug, She loved me the same in return and gave me the best life any dog could ever ask for. I was never hungry, lacked for toys, exercise, attention, love, and for that, she never lacked for my attention to her. We loved each other every day that we had together. We LOVED each other, and we showed each other what love really was. You may think it odd to speak so much of love when talking about a pet, just a pet... if you don't have this love to give... don't get a pet... please.

Do you notice a difference in me? A little age, a little weight, maybe?

The Life & Times of Dave's Saving Grace

Chapter 4

THE BEST OF TIMES
Memories matter.

Don't even think about taking it from me.

As I look back at what was my life, there were so many good times. I could never repay my mom and others for their kindness, love, care, support, and just everything that they've all done for me. Mine was a blessed life. No dog could ask for more than I was given.

I loved my treats. Even though mom tried them all, it was the soft treats that I liked. She would give me crunchy treats, and I would hide them in the yard, the furniture or anywhere I could, but they didn't go in my tummy. Her and gramma were so generous with treats. They spent money all the time on treats I liked, treats they wanted me to try, treats I would never eat. I remember even pushing them into the back seat of the vehicle. She wouldn't know for a long time.

I remember being at the cabin with mom, and grandpa and his dogs, Molly, and Dozer. His dogs are big and tough, they scared me a lot of times. One thing I did well was to get them to chase me around and then I would duck into the cabin and rush behind my mom. I was safe and grandpa wouldn't let them in to get me. I just looked at them and went about my hiding. I guess I have to admit that it was fun… a lot of fun, to get them to chase me and then to get away from them. I had to watch them close for a while after that, so they didn't retaliate when no one was looking.

One weekend, at the cabin, you won't believe what happened. I was off in the trees when I heard a coyote in the woods. I ran, and I mean ran, as fast as I could and flew into my mom's lap and there I sat for the rest of the night. We heard that coyote until we went to bed, and I was happy to do so. There are some dangerous animals that live up there. They usually stay out of the way and if they don't, I will.

Rides are a great thing. There is so much to see. A dog can hang it's head out the window and let the breeze rush over its face. I sleep a lot on rides because our rides can be very long. Sometimes we go back to a place we have been before. I like walks too, but I think the ride was the greatest, so much to see. I'm not sure if that's because I liked the place, or she did... maybe it was both. We were always headed somewhere; I never knew where and I'm not sure she did either.

The minute she opened that back gate I knew we were on our way to an adventure. When the adventure was over and we were on our way home, that's when I really slept well. I just loved the rides, we went everywhere together, right up until the end. We went on that last ride together too. The hardest ride of her life, but she did it. She was never afraid to put me in the car and head anywhere. We would stop for water or to let me pee. It didn't matter the destination. We would usually get out and walk or I might try to run around and explore the new area. I've seen the westside of Michigan so many times. We went on the beaches, up the sand dunes, in the parks, through the woods to grandpa's house we would go. She did things intentionally for the good of me. I mattered to her, and she made sure I always knew it.

I really loved the years my mom and I spent just hanging out with each other. I wasn't a dog she had for her children; I was her child. She treated me that way all my life. She loved me and we had some great days where we just lazed around and took long naps. She's like me in that way. We can sleep, long naps, she likes late mornings. I got used to it. We used to watch TV together. It was always what she wanted to watch though. We would just lay around and watch the tube.

She would let me snuggle up to her and bring a smile to her face after some moron had taken it from her. All you need is a dog, well, and a house and a job and a car and money… I guess there's a little more to it. The dog helps though.

One thing I remember loving, was my collar. It was a security thing, I guess. I just loved my collar. When mom would take it off to bathe me, or brush me, I would fight her and twist my neck and try my best to pull away. I'd bark, growl, shake my head, and she would just go ahead and take it off me. I just loved it on my neck. I felt complete with my collar on. I don't know why, really, I'm a dog, what do I know? I just know I liked it on me, and I didn't like it off me.

I wasn't really that fond of bathing. Mom was all about keeping me clean. Dogs have a way of finding a mess, dead animals, dirt, mud, you name it, we'll find it. She had this thing about me getting on her bed when I was dirty. So, I always needed a bath to get clean. The only place I like water is at the beach, off the shore. I didn't like it when gramma would try to get me to walk through the water at the shoreline. I just liked to see it, look at it, watch it, not go in it.

I always loved running through grass and fields. There aren't that many around, but I loved it when I could do it. The grass rushes through my toes and it feels great. We lived in town all the time. That meant that when we went for walks, I could and did bark at other people and dogs. I was happy to do that every chance I would get. I would never hurt anyone... maybe a cat... no, not really. I'm not a big fan of cats though. Cats just aren't like dogs. Thank goodness for that. My mom might have wanted a cat, but she chose me. That was the best day of my life.

I had a bark, a howl, and a little growl and I used all three of them whenever the time was right. Beagles are known for their howling, and mine was strong, long, and deep. The neighborhood would all hear me and that's when my mom would try to stop me, bless her heart. My mother didn't really care a lot for my barking, and howling. She used to keep the curtains drawn so I couldn't see outdoors because that's where all the action was that I would bark or howl at. She tried to minimize that as much as she could. It didn't always work out for her.

Another thing I loved was toys, mom bought me the best toys. I remember one time when she bought me a hedgehog. That stuffed toy was my best friend for the longest time, and I never took one ounce of stuffing out of it. I slept with it, I laid on the couch with it and I played with it. I loved that hedgehog. It got old, I guess, and one day it was gone. That was sad for me, I was attached to that toy. It was like I was mom's pet, but the hedgehog was my pet, and I controlled its existence, until I didn't.

I never touched the hedgehog to take its stuffing out, but after the hedgehog, the other toys were fair game. I would get a new toy and then I would proceed to remove the stuffing. Remove might be a little too nice of a word. The truth is that I would rip, pull, drag, and yank that stuffing out. It wasn't quite the same toy once I was done, but I was happy for a while. I didn't like the stuffing, or the squeaky things in the toys. But when I was done, they weren't really toys anymore. Just carcasses.

There's nothing as gratifying as pulling that stuffing out and throwing it across the room. I never stopped until the whole thing was empty, dry as a bone. Now the stuffing hadn't done anything to me, and it wasn't anything personal, I don't think. I didn't do it until I lost my hedgehog. Maybe that was my payback for that loss. It went on for years. I would pull the squeaker out, the stuffing, sometimes the eyes would come off too. There I was, left with a carcass of material. I can't say I loved the toy forever after that, but the fun was unbelievable in the moment. Small addiction on my part.

Walks were great, so great. Just slow walks, we would walk with some neighbor kids and gramma. We would stop at the library lawn where mom would bring bubbles for me and the kids to chase, we had more fun than you can imagine. Kids love bubbles, but they don't eat them like dogs do. Then there was the Coast Guard neighbor that lived next door. When I was a puppy and at my cutest point, that Coast Guard neighbor would come and get me and walk me out to the pier. The women would go crazy and swoon over how sweet, cute, and loveable I was. He would act as though I was his all the way. Where did he say I was later? Whatever, I got a walk in and that's all that counts. It was always in those walks out to the pier where I would get on those rocks by the boardwalk instead of the concrete. It was like I was in the wild trying to keep my footing on those huge rocks at the water's edge. There was so much to smell and explore in those rocks, I ran on those rocks for so many years. I heard people call her the girl with the beagle. It was like we were celebrities, like for ten people or so. It was on those walks to the pier that we were recognized.

I've talked about the beach and the sand, but I want you to understand how truly wonderful that place was for me. I loved the feel of that sand in my feet. I kind of made a little trench and then we would move to somewhere else. The beach was open, the wind was always blowing there. The waves always made soft sounds in the background while I would get my beach run on. The sand, pushing through my claws. Laying in it was always warm. I love the sun, and the breeze. I love the wind blowing through my ears and across my face. I don't have really long hair, but I could feel it pushing through and lifting until my skin would feel the fullness of the sun's warmth. I loved the heat of the sun on my coat, anytime.

My gramma loved to walk at the edge of the water. She wanted to get her toes wet. I'm not much for being "in" the water, more "at" the water. I would do it though, walk along the edge and jump around a little, but if those waves came at me, I was out of there. We would run into other dogs, and they would come up to me and then gramma would pull me away. Guess she wanted to make sure I never got hurt again. I wouldn't hurt anyone. I'm a small beagle, what am I gonna do to a big dog? My gramma has this philosophy about dogs as it relates to me and children, it goes like this: never, never, ever, put your face near a dog that you do not know. No matter how nice that dog appears, you might do something to trigger it and then it's over. She didn't care if the people said it was okay... it wasn't with her, that's final. Don't put your face in the face of an animal that you don't know really well. If you don't believe me, check out how many dog attacks are initiated that way, it'll shock you. My gramma was very serious about personal responsibility when it comes to other animals. Protect yourself she would say, don't leave it up to the stranger.

Another thing that brought me joy, please remember that I am a dog, rolling in dead animals. Yep, rolling in the carcass of a dead, rotting thing, There's nothing like it. I know how it sounds, but have you ever tried it? You should, it feels amazing. It's like a warm, mushy feeling. My mom wasn't into it like I was. That was one of the times she thought it was okay to yell at me. I would always have to get a bath, why? It felt great and it would dry. I guess I must admit that it's not for everybody. Not always crazy about a bath, that's when my collar would have to come off, and you know how I feel about someone taking my collar off. You shouldn't be mad if your dog rolls in dead things, it's just what we do. A pleasant memory, maybe if it is only for me. We got past the rolling in dead stuff thing, and she would love me again, well, she always did, she just didn't like the aftermath of the act.

My blanket was one of my favorite things in life. It made me feel safe, warm, secure, and all the good things a blanket is supposed to do. It did it. There were several blankets in my life. Some I liked better than others, but they all did the trick. You can see by the pictures that I really loved blankets, all blankets.

This guy's gonna be sorry he messed with me.

I know children have blankets too. My uncle's daughter has a blanket that our gramma gave her when she was a baby, she still has it. Nobody makes fun of her. I know my uncle has had to go back home, miles away, to get the blanket for her to sleep at night. I bet you she'll always have that blanket. Blankets are a good thing. Remember that if you have a pet. They might want their own blanket, or pillow, or something that's special to them.

Then there is the cabin and The Pines. I could tell you the whole story about the two again, but I know you know by now how much I love... desperately, love these two havens of nature that were made just for me.

There are so many things that I love to do, places I love to go, people I want to be around, but most are mom, and then gramma, and finally grandpa. Pets always, like people, like one member of the family better than the rest. The child who treats them well, the owner who loves them so much, the friend who loves to run with them. I have a lot of people in my life, most are mom's friends, but none are like her. Gramma is close, but not quite there. My mom knows me and what move I will make next.

I think that the relationship between an owner and a pet is the most wonderful thing you can imagine. I have seen dogs that have been abused and whose owners could care less for them, or about them. I hope they are all free someday. No dog, no person, no being, should have to live a life that is less than they deserve. We depend on you. Please don't misuse, malign, or discard an animal in your charge. Please. Would you like it if I did experiments on you to see which toy was best for me? Not so much fun, is it?

We were meant to be loved, just love us, that's all.

A ride is always tiring.

Blankets – who knew.

Blankets are important in life – all blankets.

The Life & Times of Dave's Saving Grace

Chapter 5

WHAT I BROUGHT TO THE WORLD

The good, the bad, and the ugly – wait a minute – I'm not ugly – the good, the bad, the beautiful me.

I'm in the best shape of my life.

You know when I first think of it, I wouldn't think I contributed all that much to the world. My gramma, she would feel different about that subject. People get pets for various reasons. They want their kids to have something to play with, to love, to care for, to grow up with. Sometimes it's to protect you or your home, to show, to breed, there are many different reasons people open their homes to animals. Still, there are some people who gain control of pets, animals, for all the wrong reasons. I'm sorry to have to say that here, but if I can take that truth, so can you. You should always do what you can to prevent or aide in eliminating such horrors and torture of animals. Maybe it's time the world thought about all the niceties and conveniences it needs that are tested on animals. Don't play that game that we need this in science. We don't need it all. If my face is beautiful without a pound of makeup, and it is, look at it, why isn't yours? Forgive me, but by nature I must stick up for animal testing/torture/dog fighting and anything else that causes unrelenting pain to my friends. We've seen it way too much over time. I'll get off my soapbox now, just think about it… please. Maybe you can make a difference. How many beagles must be tortured in the name of science.

My gramma's dad had racehorses most of his adult life. He liked them, but he raced them and if they didn't win enough, he sold them. Wow! Not sure how much commitment that really was. I guess the lesson here is that those horses were not like dogs. He had a riding stable when my gramma was young, but she said that passed fast. My gramma loves to look at horses. Her sister was really involved in all the horse stuff. My gramma, not so much.

She always keeps pictures or sculptures of horses in her house to remind her of that part of her life. Kind of like the pictures of me. She keeps a lot of them that were taken throughout my life. She just likes to look at me sometimes. She has pictures of a lot of other dogs too. She's had a lot of pets in her life. She also keeps pictures and statues of herons and cranes and egrets, and I don't think she's ever had any of those. Go figure.

Back to the subject. Long legs, mom, came to the farm to find me. I wasn't really lost; I think she was. She looked at me and fell in love with me. She took me home and my best life began. There were some hard days for both of us. But without her even saying, I think her soul looked for me and there I was. You saw the picture at the beginning. Can you really say that you could ever walk away from that? She couldn't, she didn't, and we were both better for it.

I guess what I brought to her at the beginning was distraction. I gave her lots of things to do in the beginning. It masked itself in taking care of me in all sorts of ways. The vet, training me, not really training, more of a compromise for both of us.

She was wonderful to me and so I gave her kisses and affection without any reservations. She made a home for us. She made me the center of her life. I know not all dogs have that kind of an owner, master, whatever you call it, I don't care. Long legs was like a perfect toy that you

77

would want in your life all your life, even better than my stuffed hedgehog! She was in my life and I in hers and we just enjoyed each other. We didn't have to share each other with others, so we didn't. She was the best human I could ever own, and own her I did, completely, for almost a decade and a half. What a great life this has been.

I think sometimes people must get pets for one reason and then another reason opens itself to you and another and another and before you know it this pet is immersed in your life, your family and they become a part of it all.

It wasn't just my mom who was blessed by my presence, there were others. Friends of my mom's loved me. They were mostly all kind to me and those who weren't, I was never taken around again. I brought trust in her and she reciprocated that trust to me. Sometimes, it didn't work out so well for her, but it always did for me.

I brought her a break from life when she needed it, the walks, the rides, the trips we took to long away places. I loved being in the SUV with her, she talked to me all the time. Sometimes, I would want her to shut up because I needed to rest, but she always told me what was going on in her life and how things were. We would stop and go for a walk, and she would bring the longest leash there was so I could run and run and run, beagles need exercise. She didn't always want to walk as much as I did, but she'd give in, and I would get my way for the most part. It was easy for me to get my way with her, I think I brought that to her.

How to be kind, understanding to others. She is a very kind person. I hope I helped her be that way just a little.

Dressed to the nines, eh.

I brought her a great amount of responsibility. I'm sure more than she ever wanted, or thought there would be with a dog, but she got it all. She didn't have any children and I overtook that role with ease. There were a lot of decisions that she had to make about me, for me, and she always did. She always thought of *me* when the time would come. She didn't do things to make her life easier, but mine she did. I

79

guess she brought that to me, I just gave her the opportunity to be that way. She was the kindest person you could have as a friend.

I remember playing with my uncle (mom's brother), he was nice to me. Not like my mom though. He thought she babied me, and she did. It worked out just fine for the two of us. Gramma was always on my mom's side and that was well noted throughout my life. My uncle was rough sometimes, but I could take it. Sometimes, he was a little much for me and I would tire long before he would. He'd let me rest for a while and then we'd be back at it.

He really does love me, my uncle.

After a while he had his own pet, well, it was an

actual human baby. I was in her life until she was almost eight. That little girl loved me so much, she would play with me, pet me, lay with me, just love me. I think I gave her an opportunity to fall in love with an animal. I taught her what that bond between pet and person was. We would play in my grammas backyard sometimes and I could outrun her any day. She kind of used up some of my space with gramma, but I was fine with it. Gramma would love us both without cheating either one of us, she had that much love in her for the two of us.

My uncle's child was a best friend to me. She was ready to play every time she came. She and I had a real bond with each other. She knew what I wanted to do, and she would always pet me, over, and over, and over again. I loved it and I loved her. She loved having me there and she loved me. She remembers me still and she always will.

I gave my gramma something to love when she wanted to love something again. She had suffered much loss in her life and there came a time, she needed less loss and more gain. I brought that to her. After me, that little girl would get everything that gramma had for both of us all to herself. I think that I brought that to my mom, my gramma and maybe my uncle just a little. Another view of life is often needed by someone, and a pet can fill that need. I certainly did for them. They gave me everything in return. I think I probably came out on the better end, but they would tell you they did. I guess there was enough good for all of us to catch a little.

The Life & Times of Dave's Saving Grace

As much as you may love your pet to the ends of the earth, your pet loves you more. It's a glorious feeling to have such unconditional love between two things. We are a responsibility there's no doubt. But don't think we have no responsibility in life. We have to plan just the right time to give you a kiss, to run away from you so you can get some exercise, to show you the sadness in our eyes so you will help us, and as much as anything, to give you the opportunity to love us.

My contributions were all the love I could muster to give to whoever was there for me, but mostly mom. It was to share all the fun and happy times that I enjoyed with her. She was such a great person and always had fun with me. It was to be a pet that needed to be cared for. To keep her in line when she was having a bad day, and those do come along now and then. It was to make sure she smiled at some point. To keep her safe and to make sure no stray animals came in the yard. To check the mud and dirt at The Pines to make sure it was okay for grandpa, it was. To make sure that the trails that I made at the cabin were in good shape. There were a lot of wild animals up there and they always walked on my trails and then I would come along and claim them as mine again.

My job was to snore loudly, everywhere, and anywhere I fell asleep. That way if someone else in the room snored, and many did, it wouldn't bother me. I was charged with pulling all the stuffing out of every new toy I would get to make sure mom had something to clean up.

Not until every piece of stuffing was pulled out did I really feel that this was my new toy. Yet, after the stuffing was gone, I didn't care as much for it.

I brought moments of peace and challenges of panic. I found mom's sweet spot and her bone of contention. Sometimes at the same time. I gave her a lot to do for the almost fourteen years we had together. I made her do things she didn't want to do. I let her learn how to love me fully. She let me love her deeply. She cleaned up after me when I was sick, and she comforted me after she cleaned up. I laid beside her in some of the worst moments of her life. I let her exist, always knowing I was there.

I brought fun to her. All the walks, the beach, the woods, the trails, the paths, the couch, the bed, the dog attack, the mites, the sticks, the rubbing of my stomach, the day care, the overnights while she was gone, it was all something we gave to each other. I brought trust, I brought happiness to her and others. I brought smiles to her and many more. I brought understanding to her of what it took to have a simple dog. I guess I must admit though, there was nothing simple about me. Not from the get-go.

I brought a sense of wellbeing to mom and gramma. I brought a peace when they would look in my eyes. I have beautiful eyes. As most dogs I know, we have our own personalities, just like you. You should pay attention to that, if you don't, it can overwhelm you. Like most dogs, I know how to get my way and I don't stop until I do.

The Life & Times of Dave's Saving Grace

I forced my mom to exercise and my gramma too. Neither one really wanted to, but they did. In the end, I brought exactly what a pet should, love, happiness, lessons, grief, hard times, and the most wonderful moments one could ask for in a life. I brought it all, just like every pet before me and any chosen after me. It would be nice to think that no one could live without me, but that is the great difference between a person and a pet. A person can never be replaced in the heart of the loved one who lost them... a pet can. Not really replaced, but you can feel that same excitement and love for another pet. Your heart can fill with love just as full as with another pet. My gramma says it doesn't happen that way for human loss, and from the many people she has lost, I believe her. It has nothing to do with the pet in your life, how much you love them, but another pet can come along to be loved anew, or the same, they can be owned longer and appreciated differently... and that's okay. It really is.

No matter who comes into the lives of those who loved me, it will never change the love they had for me, and still feel for me only. In the end, that's what pets are supposed to do. Make you care, teach you love, to give and receive it, bring you joy. That's what I did, and I did it with perfection for almost fourteen years.

Chapter 6

THE YEARS THEY WANE
The days they are a changin'.

**There's a lot going on out there – I should be out there.
Na… not today.**

Life began on a farm way out in the country, almost nowhere. Land, everywhere the eye could see, beautiful land. Lush grasses, the best thing to run through. It quickly took a turn to the city and then expanded into The Pines, the cabin, the beach, and a lot of other places that my mom and I went to. My gramma has been such a part of my life too. It was because of her that some of my best times were realized.

I am dripping with sweetness.

Time is passing.

Look at this profile – beauty incarnate.

Some days are just meant for laying around.

What did you think would happen with time?

I came to the world as a puppy, I grew to a young dog and now I am an old bitch. You know what I mean, an old female dog. I am so thankful for all that has been done for me. Every chance I was given to sniff for squirrels, rabbits, bugs, and every little thing that was out there for me to see and eat. Every time we traveled and every little thing I got to do; it was all so wonderful. It was so much more than I ever could have imagined, and I have a pretty good imagination.

I have found the best things in life to be, rides, walks, freedom I was given and allowed almost every day of my life. My mom was the best mom you could ever have as a dog. I'm telling you, you should all be so lucky. This is important to understand if you are a person looking to get a pet. You need to be able to put yourself aside quite often for the best interest of your pet. We are different than your children and we need your attention and protection. I guess that part is just like your children.

We are not just the *thing* that goes in the cage, the backyard or somewhere else where we can be easily forgotten and mistreated. Pets are one of the greatest joys you could have in your life. They should be treated that way. Always, no interpretation, no if's, ands, or buts. If you decide to take on the ownership and care of a pet, any kind, do your research. Make sure that the pet you decide to take on, is within your capacity to do so. I know I'm not human, but I have heard the conversations about what people do to pets... shame on you. You wouldn't like that, would you? Anyhow back to the topic at hand.

I remember the days of laying in the sun, lots of times on a chain, but there it was, the sun. The sand at the beach was the greatest thing to run through. The grass and stubble at The Pines and the cabin made me feel so young and youthful. We, as dogs, love grass to run through. The way it feels on your coat, your feet rushing through it, just the sound of it... it's great.

Where are the people who are supposed to keep me safe?

Then, I woke up one day and realized that changes were on the horizon. Once I was young and then time came to visit me. Before I knew it, life had moved me through the years. See this picture of the youth that once filled my body, so young, so vibrant. I had a youth, it was great, it was years, and it was me being the best beagle I could be.

I ran through my youth as if it would never end. Every day was something new or a repeat of something I loved to do. It seemed that any list of things I could hope for would come true. All because I had the best mom in the world. She wasn't perfect but neither was I. That's what was so great about us, we were two imperfect beings that made each other's lives so much better than they would have been had we never known each other. It is amazing how much one can affect another, good or bad, mine was always good with my mom.

There were those years in the middle. I guess those were the most vital years, where I had more energy than I knew what to do with.

What are you looking at? I'm busy here.

Here's a picture of me in the prime of my youth. I am vital and I am strong. I am a dog that has opinions and I have never been afraid to speak to them, however I could. These were the glorious days. Another thing I loved at this time of my life was winter. Where mom and I lived we had snow every year. The amount of the snow was different each year, but you can't beat running through snow piles, pushing your nose until it fills with that white, fluffy, snow. You stand up, shake your head about and snort that snow out of your nose and you're right back at it. Sometimes it's the simplest things that dogs enjoy in their lives. Sometimes it's the hardest things that they go through. There are just as many tragedies for dogs as there are for humans, ours are just forgotten or overlooked easier.

I don't remember if I fought age coming at me, I just remember that I aged. I heard my gramma once say that she turned around one day and found so much of her life was now behind her, that made her sad sometimes. She is a person who loves the moment and wishes it could last forever. I know how she feels, I feel that in my life these days.

I woke up one day and when I walked past the long mirror on the door, I noticed me, wow! I didn't recognize me at first. I'd gained a few, (more than a few) pounds. Not quite as sleek as I used to be. I didn't feel any different, I just… looked a little different.

How did all this weight get on my neck and shoulders?

My eyes are resting, that's all.

93

The Life & Times of Dave's Saving Grace

Then one day we went for a walk, just as we had so many days before, but that day it was different. It was a shorter walk, I got tired quicker. When we went home, I fell asleep very fast. When I woke up, mom was just looking at me. She smiled but I knew she was noticing something different about me. I didn't know what it was, she looked the same, the walk looked the same, the house looked the same. Why had I changed? I guess I was just maturing. As so many times before, she put her hand on my head and stroked me from my brow to my back. She bent over and kissed my head. It was like she was sad, but I didn't really get it at that moment. I would as time goes by.

I matured, and for the next few years, I found myself looking in that mirror more and more, and the changes came more frequently than before. My neck has gotten a little thicker and my belly, well, there's more of it than before. The hair around my beautiful eyes has turned a soft gray. It's still pretty but it does make me look a little more distinguished, or older. I think distinguished is the better word here. I'm not sure there is a difference. I'll take it though. Every gray hair has come with a wealth of experience for me and my mom and others. The hair on my feet is a little grayer than it was last week. My legs still hold me up but there's more of me every day to hold up.

We still go for long drives. I still eat sticks; the sand still flows under my feet, but it all seems to be slowing down a little. The best things in life are still free and still bring a smile to my face, yes, dogs can smile too.

Tonight, we are sitting around and that's just fine with me. Mom has brought in steps, for what? She puts them by the bed and tries to get me to climb up them to get on the bed. I don't need any stinking steps; I can still jump onto the bed. She leaves the room to get something, and I decide that I am going to get on the bed... my way. Here I go, missed, here I go again, shoot, missed again.

There's something out there I need to find, it might be dead, but I'll find it.

I guess I must admit that my body doesn't work like it used to. The picture above shows just what changes have taken place. I'm older, but I'm not old. I make a go at the bed again. It's not happening. I'm not getting on this bed by jumping up there. Wait a minute, mom isn't in the room. I quickly, (almost quickly) move up those steps. She walks in and looks at me and I brush her off. As far as she knows,

I jumped. She doesn't need to know the truth.

The days seem to be slowing down a little. I've had a couple of accidents on the floor. Mom isn't mean about it; she seems very understanding. My pace has slowed, just a little, I guess my eyesight has become slightly blurred, just slightly. I pay more attention to where I am going, *or*, maybe I'm just more aware of things, that sounds good, right?

I'm happy to lay around most days. The couch is warm and comfy, a perfect place to rest and look out the window.

We're all resting at the cabin, I do it well.

The steps have become my path to bed at night or on the couch. They're mobile so they go to The Pines and the cabin with us. It makes mom feel better, so I just do it. I think she sees the gray on me and thinks I'm older than I am, or at least than I feel. I can still run, jump, and roll on the ground. It just takes a little longer and the recuperation period is longer than before. Not sure there's any way to make the progression of time stop, reverse, or even slow down a little. So, I just go with it. I don't even rip all the stuffing out of my toys anymore, at least not all of them.

I'm protecting my lamb, don't even try.

Age, climbing up steps, walking, looking out windows, breathing, dreaming, everything makes me tired these days.

Another year has gone by. I cannot deny the age on my face and the weight that has attached itself to me. I move

97

slowly now. The walks, when taken, are only a few blocks now as my sight makes me much more cautious than before. They're not the long, vigorous walks that we once took. They're slow, they're calculated to be quick and easy for my legs. They bear more weight than they ever have.

At the cabin I have come to appreciate the inside more these days. I lay on the couch and just rest. Grandpa likes to hang out too. I've spent years running around outside and making my way through these woods. I can't tell you the wildlife I've seen here. Deer, raccoons, porcupine, and those stupid squirrels. Rabbits that I could never catch, now I don't even give them a second look. Life is changing and I can deny it all I want, but that won't change that it is.

So, I have decided that I will rest, enjoy the moments I can and run if the desire can be met. I will dream, I have always dreamt. My mom talks about me running in my sleep. I am dreaming of catching all those things I have chased throughout my life. I still snore and I still eat sticks.

I've had a couple of bad visits to the vet recently. I have needed help with getting the sticks out. You don't need to know. Cleaning anal glands and other things that I'm sure some people could never do; mom does all the time now. Not with a smile on her face, but she does it anyway. If you can't do it, please don't get a pet unless you can keep a vet on retainer. You might think I would have, or at least I should have learned to not eat sticks. You do know I'm a dog, right? What goes in my mouth is not something I can control. I'm a dog... get it. I've never been able to connect the pure joy of eating sticks to the horrifying pain that can come with a bowel movement. How did I know that they were connected? Things that once never bothered me have now come to be a pest in my life. I don't care much for puppies these days either, sorry, but I don't. They always want to play and snip at my face, just like children. They're way faster than I am, but when I get a hold of them, don't worry I'm not gonna hurt anybody.

All the days of me.

I'm old today. I see it in the mirror. I can almost remember that day I sat in my grammas front yard as a small puppy, watching and learning the things I could do in life at that time. I tested the boundaries and with very little repercussions I did as I pleased. I was never a mean dog, but I had moments where I had to do more growling than I might have wanted. When mom took my toys away, tried to take my collar off, made me do something I didn't want to.

Sometimes, it's just hard these days. My feet don't move as fast, my turns aren't as sharp as they used to be. I'm slower than I've ever been. I try, I really do try, but something in me says slow down, it's time... this is so hard. Surrendering gracefully to the changing tide, to the things that are happening to me that I never asked for, it's hard to accept... but accept it or not... it's here... the finality of life is crouching up behind me like a snake and I am without any ability or effort to evade the bite that brings the poison of death. Wow gramma, that's even deep for you.

I lay around most days now. I sleep a lot. My tummy hurts more than before. I can't get on the bed anymore. Mom helps me with everything. I just can't do things for myself anymore. I have no desire to run after anything or even eat a stick now.

Gramma came to visit today. Her and mom both cried a lot. Gramma kept telling me how much she loved me and how she will miss me... where is she going? I don't want her to leave my life. She has been a big part of my life. She loves me so much, why would she leave me? She kisses my head, and a tear falls on me. Where is she going? She leaves. I'm going to sleep now.

It's a new day and mom and I are going for a ride now. I'm really tired today, I don't feel well either. She said my pain will be gone today. She must be really excited for me to get better because she's crying again. She's very talkative. Like gramma did she keeps saying she loves me. I know that. Maybe we're going to get ice cream or we're going somewhere fun. Not sure I can take much fun today. She brought my blanket so maybe we're headed to the cabin. Remember how much I love the cabin. I don't think I can run around as much as I usually do, but I can lay in the driveway in the sun. I still love the sun. Why is mom crying? We have been at each other's side for thirteen years, eleven months, two weeks, five days, and some hours, where would I go now?

We're at the vets. I must be getting a shot to make me feel better. That will be nice, to feel better again, to have all this pain gone forever, that's what mom said. I can't get on the table anymore without help. I can't really see the vet too well either, he's fuzzy. My mom is crying so hard, why is she crying, it's just a shot. She bends over and kisses me like she's never going to stop. She touches me softly with the hands that I have loved all my life, the hands who have loved me with every breath she takes. Here comes the shot... ouch! Wait... I don't wanna go to sleep... mom... I can't stay awake... I'm going to sleep now... mom... mom... mom...

It is finished.

The Life & Times of Dave's Saving Grace

Chapter 7

AND THEN YOU WERE GONE, FAR TOO SOON
Our hearts are broken forever.

What a beautiful profile... right?

Always on this stupid chain.

Oh no, my ears are a mess.

The Worlds Sweetest Dog

Gracie throughout her life as I knew her, sweet, mischievous, aging like a lady.

Life for Gracie was time, you know, the time between birth and this day.

Our sweet, loving Gracie is gone. I'm her gramma, and even though it's been some years, I'm crying just like I did that day. So let me finish her journey for her. The ride wasn't over yet. She was on her way to grandpa's. I wasn't there but I can imagine the pain that pierced my daughter's heart on that ride. I know what that ride is, I've taken it before.

In that one moment at the vet, she was gone. The vet carried her to the SUV and then began the lonely, sorrow filled ride to The Pines. Her mom took her to grandpas, who had picked a spot in the woods for her to rest peacefully, then, he buried her. She loved The Pines. She just loved it there, the woods, the dirt, the chasing, and chasing, and chasing, the freedom. Today wasn't for any of those things. Today was for healing, peace from the enemy that had invaded her body in the last few years. Today was the day her pain stopped, and ours began. All her life she had come to The Pines, so much time there, running, playing, and chasing whatever she wanted. She's there forever now, right where she belongs.

Buried at one of her favorite places in the world. A place that had been a constant all her life. A place where she was free to be a beagle. A place where her grandpa loved her. A place her mother would come to find her own peace at times. A place that was filled with nature and opportunities for her to just be a dog, a beagle. Today her suffering would end, but her legacy would live on to make a difference, and she did, she made a difference, forever.

I cannot tell you exactly what her mother felt in those moments, this is Gracie's story. I can only know that I have lost, through death, many dogs and each one tore my heart apart. Some more than others, but all did. I know how much Gracie meant to her mother. I know that her heart was broken on that day and has most likely, never healed from that moment. You must understand the depth of sorrow that the loss of a treasured companion does to one's life. Then, you bury them. That is a memory you cannot lose easily. Gracie had the best mother ever. She loved her, she cared for her, and in the end, she let her go. There is no higher display of love than letting go, and nothing causes more pain.

It's been almost five years and my heart is still as broken as it was that day. She was only a pet, but she was so much more. She came into my life through my daughter, but she was here, in part, to help my heart heal from losses. She accomplished her mission and then some.

Sometimes it's hard to know the impact that anything can have on your life until you are long past it. I think that I assumed that like with all the other pets in my life, I would miss her for a time and then be thankful for the memories. That is not what happened, not even close. I knew what the steps should be. They weren't the same this time. She was old, she was frail, she was in great pain, and now, she wasn't. It was best for her that it was over. It was time. The end of her suffering was the only thing, the only thing that was good about it. Her peace.

Dave's Saving Grace, my Gracie, had taken her final breath and been laid to rest among so many other pets in The Pines. The Pines, her grandpa's land. Twenty acres of beauty, peace and calm. A perfect ending for her. It was as it should be, but not for me, not this time.

I did not realize the true impact that Gracie had on my life. She wasn't any better than any other pet I had ever had, or anyone I knew had, just different. Different in that she had so much personality, so much spunk and energy in her youth. So much love to give, and she gave it freely. The only difference I could see between Gracie and a human was, she couldn't talk. But she sure could get her point across. She got her way almost every time, and she had a way. She could understand more than any dog I had ever known and communicated better as well.

I realized after Gracie was gone what the true value of a pet is. We see them as companions, protectors, playmates for kids, and something to feed and care for. To them we are the moon and the stars, we are their world, and they treat us as such. I pray that anyone who owns or is contemplating owning a pet, remembers that. They worship and adore their masters. No matter how little they are given in return.

I was reminded by one of my children recently that I didn't keep some pets in their youth. I never gave a dog away just not to have the responsibility anymore. There were reasons they had to leave, but that statement is true. I also think some of my reasoning may have been subconsciously from the pain I felt in my youth at the loss of each pet. Perhaps, without even knowing I was doing it, I thought I was protecting them. I didn't want my children to go through that emotion, but they did. Either way I was wrong. No matter what the reason may have been, I was wrong in some cases not to try harder. In other cases though, it was the appropriate thing to do. Giving away a pet was never done out of malice on my part. The one that makes the decision is always the one to get the blame and bear the guilt.

In my defense, I did not kill my daughter's

hamster. It got loose, crawled into the furnace run and died. I didn't have the thousands of dollars to have the runs torn apart to rescue it. It was a constant reminder of that death when the furnace came on for the first time that year. The smell wafted through the house for a couple of weeks. Eventually it was gone, and we were over that loss. Then there was the bird my daughter had that got loose. We spent hours trying to catch it. It bit her and that was it for her, it was gone.

Gracie's death left me spent. I think it was Mason that changed that in me. A dog I had whose life ended tragically and slowly. That's another story. Still to this day, I can miss Gracie in only a moment. Sometimes, you don't really have a choice in the passing of a pet on to another person, and even the best choice, is the wrong choice.

Gracie was my granddog. My daughter bought me a shirt once that said exactly that. "Let me tell you about my granddog". And how true that was. She was my friend, my sweet girl, my granddog. She sucked money from me sometimes like it was air. She changed my plans in life, and she forced me to love her unconditionally. Just as she had done for me. When my first grandchild was born, I was ready for it all, Gracie had prepared me well. Gracie changed my understanding of grace itself.

So many things about her run through my mind all the time. Here are a few: Our walks on the beach were entertaining to the others there. She would run in circles, just to run in circles. I'm not sure what she was doing, but she was so happy doing it. She wasn't that keen on the water itself and never rushed in and hedged a bit when we would get close. But she loved the sand. She loved to roll in it, run in it and lay in its warmth. She entertained many at the beach, for years.

Gracie was a dog who knew how to live. She knew what she liked and what she didn't, and she had no qualms making it clear to whoever was there. She loved to ride in the car. She loved to look out the window. She would hang out and feel the breeze as it blew her ears back. Those soft, sweet, velvet ears.

She loved her toys, but after she would tear the stuffing from them, and they were flat, nothing more than material, the love was gone. I remember the hedgehog she once had. She loved it. I think that was the only toy she never ripped the stuffing from, until she was old, and it became too hard, too much work. No matter how nice or how new the toy was, the stuffing was coming out. She loved to eat sticks. This would come back to haunt her many times in her life and would ultimately play a part in the end. She loved blankets. I have many pictures of her wrapped in a blanket. If she was watching TV with you and it was her bedtime, her bedtime was self-imposed, she would let you know that she needed her blanket. You would cover her as she lay there, and she would fall fast asleep. Sometimes if her mom had company, she would just get up and go into the bedroom and put herself to bed.

She had a way of staring at you. It was a stare that

meant she wanted something, and it was up to you to figure it out. You had better because she wasn't going anywhere until she got what she wanted, but she never wanted a lot. She was a very simple girl, and as long as you made sure she was happy; you would be too. She was very snooty about food. I know this seems to be a trait of many dogs, I guess we forget that they have taste too. Hers were hers and you were never going to change it. If she didn't like something, she wasn't eating it. That's all there was to it. She had a habit of nosing out the food from her bowl that she found undesirable. Yet she would eat dead things, go figure.

I loved to touch her ears. I think I liked touching them more than she liked me touching them. They were like silk. I would move them across my cheek and smile at the feeling of comfort they offered. For a part of her life, she was overweight. Something she and I shared, and it seemed to suit her just fine. She would still walk and try as best she could to go wherever she wanted to go and not where you thought you were taking her. She listened for the most part. There were many times though, at least with me, that she didn't want to hear what I was saying to her. She would simply ignore me. She would go about what she was doing, she would turn her head. It would often take a little bit of scolding before she would agree to give up the ghost and do what you wanted her to do.

She was happy being with people. She loved being touched and stroked. She could easily be on her own though if there was no one there willing to be her slave. If there were people about and she wanted to be alone... she was. She never had a problem walking away from the crowd. She would just disappear, and you might find her resting somewhere, or doing something you might not want her to do. All in all, she was her own being.

I am not a person who believes that animals are on the same level as humans. Sorry, I just do not believe that. I believe they are here for us. I don't in any way think that means that we can treat them anyway we want. On the contrary. I believe we are responsible to keep them in the best care we can. That being said, she was so close to stepping over that line. She could love you, manipulate you, calm you, listen to you, ease your pain, do it all. She could change your mind and irritate you to no end. She could do all of it... at the same time with ease.

In the end, it was her love and devotion, her companionship and loyalty, that made her Gracie. Grace, the most beautiful beagle I have ever seen. The most loving pet I have ever known. The most honest dog to come into my life. Dave's Saving Grace was what pets are meant to be, giving, loving, and expecting of those around her to make sure she was safe and loved. Just as you were when you were in her presence. She pulled at your heartstrings with her eyes, and made you cry when her feelings were hurt. She made her mom happy, most of the time. Sometimes it all worked out, sometimes she didn't quite get there. Whatever her purpose in this life was, she completed her assignment with stars. She was the very best companion one could ask for, and the blessing was... we were given her.

In the final moments of her life, I know she looked to her mother for hope and comfort. I know she knew that her mother would never, ever, ever, do anything that would cause her any pain or discomfort in any way. I know that her mother's touch as she slipped away, was the comfort she was looking for in the last moments of her life. She was actually in a lot of pain for some time before the decision was made to relieve her of it. Her blessing to the end was the woman standing at her side. Dying inside for what she was losing, but strong in her promise to love her and care for her to the end, and she did. Through her own pain, she made sure that Gracie's pain was managed as much as possible and when that became impossible, she removed it from her.

I can barely fathom what that last ride with Gracie was like. The loneliness, guilt, and despair that must have rested heavy on my daughter's heart. I do remember that ride once, for me, it was horrific. I couldn't breathe well on that ride. Her ride must have been much the same. She was Grace's world, and Gracie was hers. The end of the ride couldn't have been any better. After all, there was burial now to be done. She was always blessed with Gracie, and now, she was Gracie's blessing. It was through her hurt, her pain, despair, and sorrow that she had her put to sleep. Sleep, a funny way to say dead. Her dad was there to bury

Gracie. We have never really talked about that day, the vet, that ride, or that grave. It's too hard, for both of us. We both loved her, and she was something individual to each of us. I feel so sorry for her loss, and yet I feel so thankful for her time with Gracie. She was great for her, and Gracie was a blessing that she needed more than anything at the time she came into her life, and mine as well. She didn't know she needed her as much as she did, but she did. Because of her need, Gracie was given a great life. Almost fourteen years old and they were all good years. She was a dog who owned a human and gave that human the best life she could while she was here on this earth. She accomplished that goal with simplicity. Then, just two weeks before her fourteenth birthday, her mission was complete.

I recently moved to a small house in the middle of nowhere. A few neighbors, not many, but that's fine with me. One thing that quickly came to my attention when I moved in was that the couple across the street, have a four-year-old beagle, named Grace. She is by far not my Gracie, but the sweet, soft memory of my Gracie passes through my mind each time I hear her bark, howl, or walk past her to say hello, and it suits me well.

There is nothing more to say about her other than thank you, thank you for every single moment of laughter and tears. You are so precious and so treasured for what you were... perfect! My memory of Gracie is filled with smiles and the best thoughts I can muster. Her loss has been very hard for me, but her life was a gift to all who knew her. A gift that just never stopped giving until that final moment when her mother brought the peace of release to her pain ridden life.

The Life & Times of Dave's Saving Grace

CHAPTER 8

TALES FROM THE PET SIDE

And there were many.

I am including this and the next section to complete Gracie's story. You may not see that at first, but Gracie's life was part of the bigger picture. The circle of life... sorry for the cliché. The context of her story is realized through the existence of all pets that came before her. The past is what made her presence so vital and important to the future, to balance all facets of pet ownership.

The number of animals that I have owned or been a part of in my life is endless. I really mean almost endless. My family, from when I was very young, to my time with Mark, to my life with my children, has had a plethora of pets come and go and stay and come and go and, and, and...

Some were as follows: A bird that lived in a condo in my parents dining room for some time until it was killed by the dirty fingers of a friend. A bird my daughter wanted, whose stay with us went by quite fast. A hamster my daughter had who committed suicide by running into the furnace run and falling down toward the furnace. It couldn't get out; we couldn't get it out and it died and was burnt up in the fall. Sweet smell of death. A couple of cats, one that died in a double pet homicide with the hawk, Tonka, that my brother had rescued before a neighbor decided to take its life and got the cat in the process.

A dog, Lobo, half wolf, and half shepherd. He was strength incarnate. A dog with integrity and a sweetness nothing could match. A beautiful little Norwegian Elkhound that was hit on a highway we lived on while he was chasing Ace, a black mini horse my father was boarding for someone. They died side by side as they lived. They were the best buddies to each other. Two Irish Setters, four Bouvier Des Flandres, three Chesapeake Bay Retrievers, two Dalmatians, a deep black poodle, two Iguanas, (my brother used them to scare girls at school, it did). A couple of baby fox (quickly ran away). A fawn whose mother had been killed, sweetest thing in the world, Bobby. Sarah, my son's beagle, a Yorkshire Terrier, a couple of English Setters, and a partridge in a pear tree… no… not the partridge.

More horses than you can count. My father had a riding stable and after that he had racehorses for decades. I could not even try too remember the number, types and colors of horses that came and went through his barn. It was always an investment, there was just not always a return on it. As beautiful as they are, is as hard as they are to care for. There are horrific stories that came with those horses, things you would never believe, but believe me they happened. I won't scare you with the gory details. You cannot have endless amounts of an animal and never have catastrophes, it's inevitable.

A horse may be a hobby, fun to ride and groom. Ten, moving from the field to the barn in the middle of a storm, that's a danger. His heart was in his horses, and so was his wallet. In the end, neither one fared well. It made him happy though, so it was all worth it to him.

I'm sure there were other pets that I have forgotten. These pets each had their own and sometimes unbelievable story, but that's another story for another day. Well, really, it's another book for another time. The point being pet lovers are usually pet lovers and have many pets at many times in their lives. That's a good thing.

Now, I am a dog person. All that means is that I am not a cat person. It has nothing to do with any other pets. It means that I would much rather have a loving dog in my home than a holier than thou, judgmental, vengeful, curtain tearing cat. That's my prerogative and I appreciate and use it. If you are a cat lover, God bless you. I'm not a Satan worshiper because I don't like cats. I just don't like cats.

I have told you about these other animals for two reasons: to bring back your own memories and offer insight to pet ownership overall. Both are very important to keep in mind. There's a lot to owning a pet. Gracie wasn't our first rodeo, but she was one of the best, without question. Also, to offer you the memory of what you felt, and memories of what you've had. If you love pets, chances are, you've loved many in the past and will love many more in the future. Your life is enriched by that furry friend or that unusual pet that no one else would ever want to own, but you enjoy it every day. I kill mice. Truth be told, I'm scared to death of them, and they will never live in my home. Yet there's a child somewhere right now, petting that rodent with every bit of love they can muster.

We always had unusual pets along with what would be considered normal pets, every one of them has been a blessing to our lives. Seek out the blessing of a pet however you determine that to be. Enjoy, take care of, and love them every day they are with you. And then... when they are gone... remember them with a smile and a tear. Just make sure the smiles outweigh the tears.

I've had a few pets in my life. Not just with my children, but with my husband and my family when I was a child, as well as other people's pets.

So, here they are, mine, my family's, and other people's pets that have touched many hearts and brought love and memories to all of us. A number of the people in these photos are gone, the pictures break my heart at the thought of the loss, but those faces make me smile every time I see them. Many of these pets are long gone too, but the owners remember them as if they stepped through the back door this morning.

MY SWEET KRA WITH HER OCTAVIA

LYNNE & MY BEAUTIFUL MASON

SEGER

OUR GENTLE GIANT – BEAR

The Worlds Sweetest Dog

DAD ON HIS PONY

DEB, DOUGLAS & MUFFET

MOM AND HER LAST DOG

TRAINED TO a T

The Worlds Sweetest Dog

GABE

MORE GABE

AND MORE GABE

The Life & Times of Dave's Saving Grace

JULIE'S SCOUT

ZACK & YUKON

The Worlds Sweetest Dog

BABY KITTEN

RICKY'S DARLING EMMA

AARON

TOBY

THE GRUBAUGH CLAN

LILA'S ELLIE   CUJO

The Worlds Sweetest Dog

STREAKER

ZACK'S SECOND BUDDY

DAD AND PENNY IN THE 1950's

DAD WITH HIS BELOVED HORSES

The Worlds Sweetest Dog

OUR SWEET LOVELY LILLIE

DAD AND HIS TEAM OF MULES

JOY'S JAX & DES (Jax is the son of Des)

MARK'S SILLY INDIE

The Worlds Sweetest Dog

SUE MISSES RUBY EVERY SINGLE DAY

THE MAJESTIC DILLON

JUST KIDDING!

CHAPTER 9:

THE THE'S:

THE BENEFITS OF A PET

I have cried a lot while writing this book. Remembering the animals that I loved and their losses. I have also smiled, as I strolled down memory lane with the many people on my mind who were a part of all the lives of these pets. That's what pets do, create memories. I believe that the benefit of a pet is impossible to convey. It can be, they give you comfort, or they give you peace of mind, or they bring you a great exercise program. A pet, be it a dog, cat, bird, or other, will give you what you need if you let them. I know that there are studies that show the physical benefits of owning a pet but there are benefits beyond that which will never be duplicated.

The benefits of Gracie just can't be summed up in words. She went so beyond any expectations one could have of a pet. Her benefits to this world will long outlive her.

THE LESSONS OF A PET

Lessons are about taking care of something apart from yourself. They are lessons of love, giving, being responsible, letting go, and moving on. Some lessons you will never want to repeat, and some you will never want to forget. Gracie was a lesson in all the above. She wore her crown of princess well, and she never let you forget that your most valuable and important lesson was to love her, and we did.

THE LOSS OF A PET

There are many reasons why pets leave our lives. Given away, put down, and death due to illness. I have given pets away and it was better for them when I did. That reason is not always understood, but it is very valid at the time. I've had my own pet put down for no other reason than the concern for the pet only. Whichever reason is yours; you will need to deal with why. I hope you can look in the mirror with honesty once the pet is gone. I know for Gracie, her mother put aside more than a decade long relationship to end the suffering that had become her life. That is love in its purest form, in its finest hour.

Putting a pet down can mean many things. The animal is at the end of their life, it has been hurt or has hurt someone else. When you are forced to make this decision, it can be devastating. I know of a couple of animals, not mine, that have been put down just because they weren't wanted anymore, how sad. No matter the reason, it's always a sad thing.

The hardest is the reason to end the pain. You still love them. When I made the decision to have Mason put down, I was devastated, for weeks. As I have said before: to be clear, put down is a vet term for kill – sorry – but that is the truth!

It took a long while for me to come to terms with the fact that I was killing something I had loved so deeply. My only consolation in those moments was, I was easing, releasing, the suffering that had taken over his body. The worst thing I could do *to* him, was exactly what he needed to have done *for* him.

Although my daughter and I have never talked about that day with Gracie, I believe with all my heart that is what she felt that day. The responsibility to do the worst thing imaginable to your pet for your pets own good. To make the decision to bring death in order to ease immeasurable pain, that is a life changing act. There are reasons to put a dog down. Some are good, some are selfish, and some are required.

Someone I once knew, through someone else, had her dog put down because she didn't want it anymore. Every time a memory of her passes through my mind and the thought of what a sweet girl she is, it's followed by another memory. The memory of a person who decided to have her loving pet killed, just because she didn't want it anymore. Forget about giving it away, fostering it, or surrendering it to the humane society. Nope, just put it down, and she did.

Then there is the dangerous dog. Gabe was a Chesapeake Bay Retriever that we had for only two years. He lived a decade in those two years, and so did we. Truth be told, Mark should have had him put down. He showed plenty of signs of aggression. We even made a conscious decision to keep our two-year-old daughter away from him. Mark loved that dog to the end. He chose a different strategy, and that was, that he protected Gabe from ever being put in a position where he could really hurt someone. At least until that kid tortured him and let him out. Even then, he was in a cage. The kid broke the lock to antagonize him. Gabe lived a short, happy life, thanks to Mark alone.

My friend had a very aggressive dog. They had to take another route. Their dog attacked a family member, drawing blood and leaving scars. That dog dug his own grave, well, not literally, but he chose his path. Down he went. This was not an easy thing for them, but as I have in my life, you have to look at the length of time this animal could cause harm while being in your care. You have to be able to assess the good, the bad, and the need.

The ride to the vet to put a dog down has happened to a number of people that I have known. It has never been an easy ride for anybody. You have formed a lifetime relationship with this animal and sadly their lifetime has come to an end, and it is because of a decision you have made... not lightly at all. A choice that brings the end of suffering to one and a long-lasting sorrow to the other.

I talked to a good friend this morning who had to put her twelve-year-old dog to sleep this week. We only spoke a moment about it before she started to cry, then I cried because I thought of Grace. She told me that her neighbor had to put her pet to sleep as well. They both cried and talked at length about the love they had for their pets and the loss they felt and will feel for years to come.

It makes sense, you love your pet, you lose your pet, you cry. The next phone call was to my niece. She has two boxers who are so animated. They are awesome dogs, and she has had them for a long time. In our conversation she told me that she had recently had to put her white boxer to sleep. He was nine and had medical issues that could not be cured. More tears from both of us. That boxer was so handsome and was an extremely sweet and loving dog. I really liked Jax. He made many years of her life great. She is a wonderful pet parent and now has her own granddog.

There is no amount of words that can heal the heart of a pet owner at that moment. You want to do anything you can to save them, keep them, and then when you can't do anything… you must let them go and then… you cry, and cry, and cry some more. Then one day, you think of all the wonderful things they brought into your life, and you smile, then you cry again. You'll smile again soon at the thought of them.

Put to sleep, doesn't that sound sweet? A nap, rest, not

quite. Put to sleep, put down, whatever you call it, it is death, loss, and pain. No other way to say it and anyone who has ever had to make that decision knows without question how that event unfolds in your life. Keep the memories, let go of the pain, and get another pet.

THE CHOOSING OF A PET

Of course, you need to know what pet you want, a dog, a cat, a guinea pig, a horse, a fish, a bird, ferret, the choice is endless. Research the care of the animal you want. That could be very important in the long run. Certain types of animals are prone to certain diseases or afflictions. There are breeds of dogs that might have kidney issues, hip dysplasia, leukemia, and a plethora of other conditions that will cost you money, time, and possible heartache in the end.

The number of dog breeds to choose from are endless. Bouvier Des Flandres, Vizsla, Rhodesian Ridgebacks, Chesapeake Bay Retrievers, Poodles (all three sizes), Yorkies, Irish Setters, Norwegian Elkhounds, Basset Hounds, Bloodhounds and the like. Water dogs, bird dogs, hunting dogs, sporting dogs, show dogs, leader dogs, anything your heart desires.

Take the time to enjoy, train, and care for the pet you choose. They have no one else but you to turn to and they will depend on you all their life. The time you will spend with your pet will be either good or bad, easy or hard. It is completely up to you. You can make it a chore or a blessing, whichever you choose. Do yourself a favor, just take the time to make it matter, because whether you like it or not, it will matter. It's up to you how much it will matter, but it will.

The one thing all pets have in common is that they need care, cost money, and require your love and attention throughout their whole life. Puppies always grow into dogs who grow into old dogs, kittens grow into cats, all lives go through a process of baby, to teen, to old, and then to death. The death part is the part you have to acknowledge, because no matter how much you wish it won't come to your pet, it will, just like it will to you.

Take the time to do the research to make sure the fit, the cost, the time investment, and everything else involved is something you are willing to take on… and then take it on!

THE MEMORY OF A PET

I have memories of certain pets over others. I am not sure if it was my age or the relationship with the pet that created stronger memories than others. I do know that my life is so much better for every pet that I have ever owned. When it comes to Dave's Saving Grace, that is a memory that I relive so often and so fondly, and always will. The memory of her makes me smile, laugh, cry, and thank God for her. She was worth it.

THE VALUE OF A PET

I don't think you can measure the value of a pet in one's life. They bring joy, lessons, and companionship that some children would never have without them. For seniors, they are lifelines and for all ages in between, they offer a wealth of emotion, happy and sad, that you will never find anywhere else. Lessons and commitments that you will fulfill with gladness. Gracie cost my daughter one hundred twenty-five dollars. Her value though, was easily beyond a million dollars as far as I'm concerned.

THE PURPOSE OF A PET

To address the aforementioned and following points, which is the purpose of a pet. Not to be abused, mistreated, or neglected. A pet is what brings unconditional, non-threatening, innocent love to your life. **The fit is the *key*.** You need to connect with something that will be in your life for years to come. Seriously, years to come. Gracie's fit was perfect, for my daughter, for me, for her grandpa, and all others she touched, just perfect.

THE COST OF A PET

A lot... I mean a lot. Check this out before you make the decision to have a pet. With Gracie, in one year I spent seven hundred dollars, and didn't even own a pet! That wasn't the attack, that was vet bills, shots, help with food, toys, daycare, boarding, and treats only. There are shots,

142

emergencies, annual care, toys, food, daycare, and things of which you will never even think of ahead of time that will cost *you*. Understand, even free pets aren't really free.

There is a cost. Mark and I, and I with my kids, have spent thousands on pets. There have been many dogs, many emergencies, tragedies, and beyond that each came at an expense to the owner. Beyond food, there are many costs that seem to come from nowhere. Emergencies, like over four hundred dollars for the attack on Gracie - five hundred dollars Bear's broken leg - one thousand dollars Gabe's autopsy - two thousand dollars Gabe's drag incident - one thousand dollars to poison Lillie - sixteen hundred dollars to care for the end of Mason's life – well over a thousand dollars for the court case to free Gabe. Another thousand dollars or more on the crayfish diagnosis for Gabe. There's not enough room for all the others. The emergencies my father paid for in the care of his horses is astounding. His cost over the years was tens of thousands of dollars. Were they all worth it? Every single one was to him. He cared for his horses like I care for dogs, the right way.

THE CARE OF A PET

This is big if you ask me. General care, things that arise. Safety, grooming, emotional (yes, I said emotional), a plethora of things will come with this. Most, you'll never see coming. They will keep you moving throughout their lives. Gabe's drag emergency, Bear's leg, Lillie's poisoning, these events took more than money. They took time to care for, and time to heal. Mason's life after the accident was day by day, then hour by hour, then minute by minute, right up to the end. Gracie's care was magnified in the last months of her life. Pets aren't a walk in the park, they're a journey to the mountain top and then through the valley.

THE EXPERIENCE OF A PET

The experience of a pet is as individual as a snowflake. I have had dogs that have been a chore to own and yet I have enjoyed them immensely. I have had pets that have been riddled with tragedy and barely found the time to breath between each emergency that arose and yet those pets have taught me lessons I have used throughout my life. I have had pets that friends may have thought I should be rid of, yet that experience has filled me with emotions that I am so thankful for. They've all been great experiences.

I suppose the experience of a pet is something only the pet owner can understand, as it should be.

THE LOVE OF A PET

This is a two-way street. Pets start by giving love unconditionally. Yet as some do to their children, they can be taught to hate and distrust if you impress those lessons on them enough. They will never ask for anything negative, it will be your choice only to give it to them. This does not mean that there may be pets that are not the right fit – that's on you to take care of – not your pet. There was never one moment that Gracie didn't love, even when she didn't want to.

I have seen so many animals just adore their owners. It's the cheapest love you can have. You can yell at them, ignore them, and they will kiss you in a moment. They forgive quicker than you can turn your head. Unfortunately, they will endure a lot of cruelty and still love you. Please, treat them as they deserve to be treated.

THE REALITY OF A PET

They can be everything you want them to be. They will love you, pee on things, throw up on things, and kiss you right after. They will know when you need love. They will fear you when you show hatred or anger toward them. They are going to chew, probably your most treasured things, scratch, and dig. Not at the same time, and not in that order, but it will all be done. They will cost you more than you would ever believe, in money, time, and affection. They are a wonderful thing to bring into your home, at the right time. There is nothing better than the love of a pet and there is nothing sadder than the loss of one. There is nothing worse than the abuse of one either. Please choose to be on the right side. My daughter gave Gracie the best life any dog could want. Gracie made us all better people. The richness of our lives is often created by our pets.

THE COMPANIONSHIP OF A PET

There is nothing, not even parenthood itself, that compares to a pet as a companion. There are many reasons one might want or need a companion, and a pet can certainly fill that need with ease. The only thing I would suggest is that you read all the pages before this one first. Although a pet can be the greatest thing in your life, it has cost, and many other aspects that should be considered. At this time in my life, I would love to have a pet. I am a big dog person; I love big dogs. As a senior though (they say it, not me), I don't feel that I could handle a big dog like I have in the past. I am contemplating a smaller dog, but I have been contemplating that for a couple years now. I know the benefits, but I also know the cost. There is a monetary cost as well as going outside when it rains and snows. Going to the vet, puppy training, cleaning up and buying dog food and treats and blah, blah, blah. I'm not a patient person, so I struggle with my impetuous nature to just go get a dog. I haven't yet, I don't know if I can, or will. I hope I will. Maybe someday, but not today. One nice thing for me is my new house. Right across the street from that beagle named Grace. She resembles my Gracie in the prime of her life. Her markings aren't as colorful as my Gracie's, but she's still very pretty. She makes me think of Gracie, same mouth, I mean barking all the time, like beagles do. It doesn't bother me though, not in the least, because in every bark, or growl at the squirrels, I relive a memory of my Gracie as it washes across my mind, and I

146

smile. I always smile.

I hadn't remembered all the pets that passed through my life until this book. Thank you to Gracie for all these memories. I am so melancholy these days, but going back, remembering pets and family and times with all of them, it reminded me of how rich my life has been with both tragedy and blessings galore. I wouldn't trade a moment to make things better if I had to lose one memory. Please take a few moments and look back at the abundance of pet memories in your own life. No matter your age, it's all there, look. They are so wonderful to have, so much work to take care of, and so missed when they are gone. Anyone who has ever had a pet in their life is blessed beyond measure, and they will tell you so with great pride in their pet.

IN ADDITION:

I am going to add a checklist to this chapter. It is by no means the end all of checklist. These are ideas that may create other ideas, questions, understandings of what one should think of when contemplating the addition of a pet to your home, family, apartment, or wherever you may live. Any type of pet, bird, dog, cat, iguana, ferret, hedgehog, spider, hamster, snake, fish, any, any, any. Please review and *think* before you decide. That decision will cost you in some way and you may never even see it coming.

PET CHECKLIST

- Do your research, pet type, what breed?
- Is your home ready? Poisons, chewing?
- Are you willing to be outside in the wind, rain, snow, and any other conditions?
- Is someone going to feed it every day?
- Is your wallet thick enough to handle it? Vet bills, emergencies, toys, food...
- Are your children on board, completely?
- Is there time to spend with a pet, train?
- What about when you go on vacation?
- Are you able/willing to pay for daycare?
- Can the size of the pet go with you everywhere you visit, vacation?
- Have you reviewed the safety issues of a pet (both for and from the pet)?
- Do you know the life expectancy of the pet – they will usually die before you or your children, ready for that?
- Is your lifestyle open to a pet?
- Are you willing to go thru and pay for obedience training?
- Can you emotionally, physically, and financially handle emergencies?
- Anybody allergic to anything?
- Is your homeowner's insurance up to date? Make sure it is.
- And all the other things that will come up.

Chapter 10

FINAL THOUGHTS

**I enjoyed my life, really, I did. I gave so much to so
many and received the same. I hope your heart enjoyed
my story and your pet has the best life ever, just like I
did. Thank you, mom. You were the best human I could
have ever owned.**

And even though Gracie has become the most

endearing pet I have known – there were others. There should be others. Anyone who loves pets should never own just one.

Dave's Saving Grace was exactly and always what a beagle, a pet, should be. She was loving, cared for, unconditional, and never abused. She brought countless people smiles, laughter, tears, and good memories. She taught lessons you never knew you needed. She was never judgmental and always willing to lick your face or let you hug her... and hug her we did, for almost fourteen years.

She was just a beagle puppy who turned into a life saver for more than one person. She was a dog... a friend... a granddog... a funny little puppy, whose light will shine forever in more than one heart.

Her ears were so incredibly soft, like velvet. The best thing in the world to rub against your face. I used to tell her that when she died, I was going to make a purse out of her ears. There were two reasons I would say that, first, because they are so sweet and soft, and second, because I knew she would die someday, and I loved her more than any animal I had ever known. I used to tell her my heart would break when she left... it did... and it still is broken when it comes to Gracie.

Her eyes were so innocent, which she was not, not in any way. She could get away with anything and always tried your patience just before she melted your heart. I loved that dog, and I always will. She loved so many and gave so much more than she ever asked for. She made a difference.

That is what a pet should do. Make a difference in your life. She was a gift, and that's what a pet should be. Not tortured, not abused, not neglected, not an experiment, but loved, appreciated, understood, thanked for everything, and most of all, enjoyed to the very end. She was everything, she was, to the very end. Thank you.

Please feel free to give us an honest review on Amazon or tell a friend. We want Gracie's life to count. In this world today, it should. We truly appreciate any help to share her story, funny and sad, it's worth taking the time to read. Thank you, Gracie, and gramma.

ARE WE THERE YET?

Yes, my sweet darling Gracie, we're there. You're gone,
but we got there, in part because of you.
Thank you.
Rest peacefully, you deserve it.

Made in United States
Orlando, FL
23 March 2025

59737012R00085